When someone meets Mary Margaret, the ⬚⬚⬚⬚⬚
She is one of the most engaging young le ⬚⬚⬚⬚⬚
of working with and when you begin to re ⬚⬚⬚⬚⬚
realize you, too, have a new friend. Mary ⬚⬚⬚⬚⬚ *you*
on in your calling to bring teen girls closer to Christ, and she'll show you
how to make an eternal difference in the next generation.

—KELLY KING, LIFEWAY WOMEN'S MINISTRY SPECIALIST

Women can be quick to disqualify themselves from
mentorship (or even relationship) with younger women, but
Mary Margaret's words assure us we don't have to know any
secret handshakes or catchphrases to effectively teach and
model what it looks like to live a life surrendered to our Savior.

Grounded in Truth, Show Her the Way is reassuring, practical, helpful,
encouraging, and challenging—a guide for women of any age who want
to pour into the generation behind them but aren't sure where or how to
start. Without a doubt, this is a book I'll enthusiastically recommend over
and over again.

—SOPHIE HUDSON, AUTHOR OF GIDDY UP, EUNICE AND CO-HOST OF THE BIG BOO CAST

I have personally seen how Mary Margaret combines a love for
discipleship and a love for students into a practical ministry that presents
in conversations, service projects, and overall organized fun. She is able
to tell her story in a way that both inspires and challenges, especially if
the reader will take the time to reflect on the suggested questions and
discussion starters that are carefully included throughout the book.

—DR. R. ALLEN JACKSON, PROFESSOR OF YOUTH EDUCATION AND COLLEGIATE MINISTRY AT NEW ORLEANS BAPTIST THEOLOGICAL SEMINARY

Mary Margaret is not only a great friend and leader in the world of student ministry, but also has the ability to inspire and challenge anyone to pursue Christ more wholeheartedly. She encourages us to make discipleship a part of our everyday lifestyle and calling as a believer. It's such an urgent, yet simple calling on the lives of us all. Her heartbeat for the Lord is literally felt through every page and motivates all of us to intentionally invest into the lives of teen girls.

—STEPHANIE WILLIFORD, DIRECTOR OF
GIRLS' MINISTRY AT PRESTONWOOD BAPTIST CHURCH

In Show Her the Way, Mary Margaret breaks down daily discipleship by looking to the life of Christ. She offers practical tools, strategies, and wisdom to equip women to come alongside girls in their journey of following Jesus. Above all, Mary Margaret gets to the heart of discipleship and breaks it down to one simple, profound truth to remember: point her to Christ. One thing I can guarantee, you'll walk away from reading Show Her the Way with a fire in your bones to go and reach the next generation of girls with the life-changing gospel of Jesus Christ!

—GRETCHEN SAFFLES,
FOUNDER OF WELL-WATERED WOMEN

This book operates on multiple levels clearly articulating the need and a focused strategy for doing the work of girls ministry and making disciples that will fundamentally impact the trajectory of culture. Mary Margaret clearly teaches that relationships are the greatest classroom for discipleship. I highly recommend this book for anyone who desires to be intentional about developing young ladies to turn the world upside down for Jesus!

—BRENT CROWE,
VICE-PRESIDENT OF STUDENT LEADERSHIP UNIVERSITY

MARY MARGARET WEST

SHOW HER THE WAY

LifeWay Press®
Nashville, Tennessee

STUDENT MINISTRY PUBLISHING TEAM

Director, Student Ministry
BEN TRUEBLOOD

Manager, Student
Ministry Publishing
JOHN PAUL BASHAM

Editorial Team Leader
KAREN DANIEL

Content Editor
MORGAN HAWK

Content Specialist
JENNIFER SIAO

Graphic Designer
SARAH SPERRY

ISBN: 978-1-5359-2534-1
Item Number: 005807929

Dewey Decimal Classification Number: 230.007
Subject Heading: RELIGION \ CHRISTIAN MINISTRY \ YOUTH

Printed in the United States of America

Student Ministry Publishing
LifeWay Resources, One LifeWay Plaza, Nashville, TN 37234

We believe that the Bible has God for its author; salvation for its end; and truth, without any mixture of error, for its matter and that all Scripture is totally true and trustworthy. To review LifeWay's doctrinal guideline, please visit www.lifeway.com/doctrinalguideline.

TABLE OF CONTENTS

ABOUT THE AUTHOR

 **MARY MARGARET WEST** serves as the Girls Ministry Specialist for LifeWay Christian Resources, which basically means that teen girls and the women who lead them are her favorite people on the planet. She has a passion to equip girls and women to dive deeply into God's Word and live out their calling. Mary Margaret is a former Girls Minister and holds a master's degree from New Orleans Baptist Theological Seminary. Mary Margaret is married to Jonathan and they love living in Franklin, TN.

DEDICATION

For my Mom, Shugie Collingsworth, more than any other woman in my life, you have consistently pointed me to Jesus and have shown me the way. To the countless women who have discipled me over the years, I am forever grateful for the impact you've made on my life. Know that I'm carrying the torch to the next generation because of your faithfulness. To the Dream Team, thank you for believing in me and teaching me how to minister to students. To Michael Smith, your legacy of loving and leading students lives on in me. To my prayer warriors, this book would still be in my head and heart without you. To Jonathan, thank you for loving me as I am and cheering me on as we follow God's call on our lives together.

INTRODUCTION

Hey, friend! I'm so excited that we're about to walk together on this journey of discipling teen girls. Throughout this book, you'll find ideas, resources, and tools to help you as you disciple teen girls. You will have the opportunity to write your own answers and strategies so that by the time you're done, you will have created your own map to show girls the way. Some of you are going to do that one-on-one and others are going to disciple a group of girls. Many of you are going to disciple in your home, and some are going to set up a structured way to disciple, whether it be through your church or on your own. You may wonder, "Is this the right way to disciple?" Friend, the answer to that question is a resounding "Yes!" If you're being obedient to God's call on your life by discipling the next generation, do what He's calling you to do without comparing yourself to anyone else.

You'll find a lot of next steps as you read. I hope you'll hear my advice and just take those steps one at a time. Give the Lord opportunity to show you which way to go, and be obedient to Him as you continue to walk this out. Even if you've never been formally discipled, you have what it takes to disciple a teen girl. If you're walking in relationship with Christ, you can do this. As we journey together through these pages, know that I've prayed for you along the way. I've prayed that God would use this as a tool and resource to point both you and the girls in your life to Jesus.

Are you willing? If you're reading this, I'm guessing you are. Friend, that's what it takes. As you continue to read this book, be teachable. Be ready. Pray that God would open your heart and give you what you need to carry out the calling He's placed on your life to disciple younger women.

CHAPTER 1

DISCIPLE HER

No matter what stage of life you're in, you have something to offer a woman younger than you.

"Can you pray for my friend's cat? She's really sick." My jaw really wanted to hit the floor, but I couldn't let it. An eighth grade girl in the small group I had just committed to lead asked me to pray for her friend's cat. What I didn't expect was the onslaught of cat prayers that were to follow that day, and every other Sunday for a few months. I was a junior in college and had prayed that God would give me an opportunity to serve at my church and felt like I could probably handle student ministry. Our junior high pastor needed someone to teach eighth grade girls, so I very sheepishly said yes. I'd never done anything like this before. When I felt like God was prompting me to serve in student ministry, I thought I could check the roll on Sunday mornings or hand out pizza. I had no idea God was going to plop me in the middle of a bunch of cat-loving eighth grade girls every week to teach them about the Bible. I realized very quickly how teachable these girls were and how much God was using this opportunity to teach me at the same time. I can honestly say this group of girls was really pivotal in my walk with Christ, and I've never been the same. As you journey through these pages, I'm praying that God would use these stories, Scriptures, and strategies to clarify your call to love and minister to teen girls. I'm praying their lives would be changed for the glory of God, and that yours would be also.

Discipleship isn't easy. For me, it started in some ways as a three-year-old at home, and it's been a continual journey throughout my life. My mom is the one who helped shape so much of my spiritual life. As a woman, she's set an incredible example for me, and she has allowed other women to speak into my life, and a lot of that is because of the women who spoke into hers.

"I don't want to ask Jesus into my heart because I don't want anyone telling me what to do." That was me, age three, talking to my mom. At the time, she was a student pastor's wife and was counseling a teen girl at our kitchen table. Little Mary Margaret overheard most of the conversation, and that was my response. I've always been strong-willed, but there was no doubt after this incident. My mom talked to me later about what I said, but I knew I didn't want anyone bossing me around.

Here's the good thing, y'all: Jesus isn't trying to boss you around. His aim isn't to tell you what to do, but to guide you into obedience. This whole thing is about relationships—and the same goes for discipleship. As women, we've got to make time to build relationships with the women in the next generation. It won't happen by accident, but it always bears fruit, whether or not we ever see it with our own eyes.

Once a year, my mom's friend Mrs. Ethel asks her to come and lead a devotional at the retirement home where she lives. She's ninety-six years old and was one of my mom's small group leaders when she was just twenty-four. In my mom's words, "She was willing to take on our small singles group." My mom loves to spend time with Mrs. Ethel because she's wise, and she's been a faithful friend and discipler of women over the years.

Whether you're a mom of a three-year-old who's beginning to understand and learn or you're ninety-six and have lived a full life of giving your life to others, you have something to bring to the table. Some of you are new to discipleship and others have been actively discipling for years, but don't let that hold you back from whatever next step God means for you to take in discipleship.

Throughout Scripture, we are all called to be disciple makers. In the Bible, some things are mandates. We see Jesus give a mandate to believers after His resurrection in Matthew 28:

> *Go, therefore, and make disciples of all nations, baptizing them*
> *in the name of the Father and of the Son and of the Holy Spirit,*
> *teaching them to observe everything I have commanded you.*
> *And remember, I am with you always, to the end of the age.*
> –Matthew 28:19-20

Discipleship isn't optional. As a woman, you are called to invest in younger women. As we launch into talking about discipleship, let's give the word some clarity.

How do you define discipleship?

A disciple is a student or a learner. Merriam Webster's dictionary defines it as, "one who accepts and assists in spreading the doctrines of another: such as Christianity: one of the twelve in the inner circle of Christ's followers according to the Gospel accounts."[1] When you go back to the original text of the Bible, the Greek uses the word mathētēs, which is defined as "a learner, i.e. pupil."[2] That same word is used over 230 times in the New Testament. Is it just me, or have we made discipleship sound scary and intimidating?

How does your answer compare to what the dictionary says?

Disciples spend time around those they want to learn from.

Who are you learning from, and who's learning from you?

And they spend time learning about things they are interested in.

We're all students of something. What are you studying?

YOU CAN DO THIS

In the Book of Philippians, we see Paul and Timothy's relationship play out in a unique way. These two men spent years and years doing ministry alongside each other, and we see it happening through the pages of this letter to the church at

Philippi. Paul took Timothy with him while he was doing ministry. In the two letters that bear his name, Paul addresses him first as, "Timothy, my true son in the faith" (1 Tim. 1:2), and then as, "Timothy, my dearly loved son" (2 Tim. 1:2). Paul writes of Timothy in Philippians saying, "Now I hope in the Lord Jesus to send Timothy to you soon so that I too may be encouraged by news about you. For I have no one else like-minded who will genuinely care about your interests ..." (Phil. 2:19-20). He sees Timothy as like-minded and knows he can carry out the work that is before them. Paul finds in Timothy someone to share his life and ministry with.

In the same way, Timothy makes himself available and teachable. He has spent the better part of his life doing ministry alongside Paul, but he's still learning. He's put himself in a position to lead and learn at the same time. I wonder if Timothy knew Paul was preparing him to be unleashed to do the same thing he had always watched. I'd love to ask him if he realized what a big deal Paul would be to countless generations of Christians. Timothy had a seat at the table to learn and so do you. We live in a day and age where we have access to more resources and people than ever before. Are you utilizing the resources around you and the people you can learn from?

Here's the deal. In this scenario, you're not Paul—you're Timothy. It's easy to be discouraged because we don't know it all, and we think we have to be like Paul when it comes to discipleship. Paul was the expert, but he was so genuine in the way he taught and led. He knew what he was doing, he was passionate about doing it, and he was leading and living well. What we learn from their relationship is that everything Paul was teaching was in preparation for Timothy to be sent out to do the same. You probably picked up this book because you are ready, or someone picked it up and handed it to you because they believe in you. You're at the point of taking the next step. Someone has invested in you, and now you're ready to turn around and invest in someone else. Maybe you've been discipling younger women for years and you're looking for some fresh ideas and strategies. Or maybe you know God is calling you to disciple a younger woman, and you're trying to figure out what that looks like.

THE TIME IS NOW

We need to make investing in teen girls a priority because they are the future, the next generation, and the legacy we will leave behind. Now that I'm in my mid-thirties, I'm realizing more than ever that I'm not always going to be the "younger woman." At a conference I recently attended, they asked how many of us considered ourselves to be the younger woman and the older woman. I honestly wasn't sure which one to raise my hand for! What I do know is I constantly need to be learning and leading. I need someone ahead of me, as well as someone behind me. We all need people like this in our lives. You never know how those girls may enter your life. Some of you have been feeling a tug toward discipling a particular girl for a long time, and others are beginning to pray you'll meet her soon. Whatever circumstance you find yourself in, remember the time is now. Keep your eyes open!

In the life cycle of the local church, Promotion Sunday is one of my favorite days of the year. It's when all of the age-graded kids and students move up to the next grade, and there's this fun shift that happens as you watch them take their new places. I'll never forget one Promotion Sunday when I stood at the front door of our student ministry building greeting students and parents as they arrived. We had an influx of new sixth-grade students, and they were easy to spot. One girl in particular lasted about five minutes before the tears started to run down her cheeks. One of our student pastors asked me to go talk to her (if you haven't noticed, a lot of men don't know what to do with tears), so I crouched down and introduced myself to her.

"I'm Mary Margaret, and I work in student ministry. What's your name?"

"I'm Emily," she said with clasped hands and a quivering chin.

"Emily, we're so glad you're here today. Is everything okay?"

"Nooooo..... it's just too much. I don't like having to walk across the parking lot, and it's too much change all at once. I still haven't even figured out how to open my locker at school yet." (cue ALL the tears)

Emily and I sat down and talked for most of that Sunday morning. I had a lot of other things I needed to be doing, but Emily took priority. I asked her what she did over the summer, and she told me about visiting her grandparents in Mississippi and going to camp. She told me her parents' marriage wasn't in a good place and that sixth grade didn't sound very exciting—she missed fifth grade and the comfort she knew before lockers, changing classes, walking across the parking lot at church, and so many other things came into the picture.

I have to admit, I'm not the most empathetic woman on the planet. I'm pretty factual and have a hard time putting myself in other people's shoes to better understand what they're feeling. While I'm talking to people, I'm coming up with a list of solutions to their problems in my head and usually love nothing more than telling them what to do (true confessions, friends). That day, I knew I had to sit and listen. I had to remind myself of what it was like to be in the sixth grade where everything changed all at once.

I remembered sixth grade, and the biggest way I saw all this change happening was when my best friend, Jennifer, had me paged to the guidance counselor's office during school. She wanted to tell me she had found a new best friend named Kyle, and she didn't need me anymore. I was devastated. We'd been best friends since first grade, and I felt like the rug had been pulled out from under me.

I thought of everything I could remember from my sixth-grade year to help put myself in Emily's shoes that day and let her know that yes, things were changing, but she could do it. She was brave and strong, and she wasn't going to have to do it alone. I told her we could talk anytime she needed to.

Over the next few weeks, I sought Emily out at church and asked how things were going. I wanted her to know I hadn't forgotten what she shared with me that day. I wanted her to know I was praying for her. After a while, she walked in the door confidently because she was starting to figure things out on her own. She made friends in her small group, and it wasn't so hard anymore to walk across the parking lot.

FOLLOW HER LEAD

The women who have discipled me over the years have made a profound impact on my life. When I was in seventh grade, Judy Toler (also known as "Grandma Toler") was my Sunday school teacher. All of the seventh-grade girls hoped and prayed that when we found out what class we would be in for the year, it would be her class. She was old enough to be our grandma, but she was the cool version who had sleepovers at her house and always went to youth camp each summer. She loved Jesus, her family, and seventh grade girls. Did she dress like us? Nope. Did she know what we were talking about half the time? Probably not. What she did do was invite us into her home. We had a talent show, ate junk food, and had so much fun together. She was (and still is) a faithful prayer warrior for the girls in her class. Last time I asked, she was still going to youth camp. Grandma Toler taught us about Jesus, and she lives it out by serving and investing in the lives of teen girls over the course of decades.

When I was a high school student, Shannon (my student pastor's wife) asked me to be a part of a discipleship group she led on Wednesday nights. There were about twelve girls in the group, and over the course of the school year, we studied the Bible and memorized Scripture together. One year, we walked through 1 & 2 Timothy together, and the next year, we used Beth Moore's book *Praying God's Word* as our discussion and study guide. I'm so grateful for Shannon and that group of my peers I was able to grow alongside. Spending time in the Bible with other girls my age helped me realize how much I still didn't know and understand about Scripture, but it also gave me a really safe place to ask all of my questions.

Oswald Chambers' *My Utmost for His Highest* is one of my favorite devotional books. I love the way he talks about discipleship:

> *Jesus did not say to make converts to your way of thinking, but He said to look after His sheep, to see that they get nourished in the knowledge of Him. We consider what we do in the way of Christian work as service, yet Jesus Christ calls service to be what we are to Him, not what we do for Him. Discipleship is based solely on devotion to Jesus Christ, not on following after a particular belief or doctrine ... A person touched by the*

Spirit of God suddenly says, "Now I see who Jesus is!"—that is the source of devotion. Today we have substituted doctrinal belief for personal belief, and that is why so many people are devoted to causes and so few are devoted to Jesus Christ.[3]

A life devoted to Christ is one people can follow. We're not asked to be perfect, but to be willing and devoted. It's so easy to take a stand for what we believe on Twitter and Facebook, but what does it look like when it plays out in our day-to-day lives? We often forget that discipleship begins and ends with Jesus Christ. He's not our best friend or homeboy; He's our Savior. He's not a cause to follow, but He lived a life worthy of following. Obedience to God superseded anything else that came into play in His life. When we devote ourselves to Jesus, we'll be leading others. We'll be discipling those behind us.

STAY FOCUSED

Discipleship doesn't look the same on everyone. Here are some baseline questions to think about:

What has discipleship looked like in your life?

Are there girls or young women who ask if they can spend time with you?

Do you make yourself available?

Whatever you do, don't look to the right or left all the time and compare your discipleship journey to that of anyone else. Your story is unique. The story God is writing in your life is unlike that of anyone else. For some women, discipleship looks like a program with a lot of structure. Maybe that's you, but maybe it isn't. The goal is to figure out why it's important and how you're going to tackle it.

Why is all of this so important? Why did you pick up a book about discipling the next generation of girls? It's because it's what we're called to do. Throughout the New Testament, we are called to live as examples. Just like we saw Paul charge

Timothy to be an example and lead others, he made several charges throughout his letters to churches. For example, First Corinthians 11:1 says, "Follow my example, as I follow the example of Christ" (1 Cor. 11:1; NIV). Paul is telling the believers they can follow him as he keeps his eyes fixed on Christ. Theologian N.T. Wright makes a great point in reference to this passage:

> Paul reminds them of the basic rule of life which he knew he was giving them when he was with them. He always tried to do what was best for others, not for Himself, and in that he had been copying the Messiah himself (see Rom. 15:2-3). They must now learn to copy him. If all Christian teachers had it in mind that their hearers were also observers, and that the lessons they learned with the eye would be the ones that would go deepest, the gospel might have advanced further and faster.[4]

Wright makes a great case for why discipleship is crucial to believers. Discipleship does not just mean we teach, but we lead with our very lives. Those we disciple are not just hearers, but observers. They are watching to see why and how we do everything we do, and our lives become a testimony to what we believe. This can be incredibly intimidating, but when we keep our focus on Christ, He is the one on display, not us. He is the one they are ultimately looking to—we just have to be honest with where we are in the process.

Teen girls need to know it's worth it. Jesus is worth everything. Discipleship is important to us because it's important to God. They need your wisdom and experience. They need to hear that life isn't always easy, but God is always faithful. They need to see you faithfully walking out your calling. They need to see that you're not perfect and you don't always get it right, but you're still learning and growing. It's critical for them to see that spiritual health isn't equated with perfection, but with imperfection and a passionate pursuit of Jesus Christ. They need to know it's okay to mess up, but it's important to repent and move on. They need to see that forgiveness isn't optional.

Girls aren't looking for you to be perfect, but they're looking to you to point them to Christ. As a woman who believes in Jesus, you are called to disciple other women. Your calling looks different than that of anyone else, so what you have to offer is needed.

Spend a few minutes writing out what you believe God has called you to do in this season of your life when it comes to discipling girls.

I'm at the point in life where I'm not always the younger woman. I'm thirty-four, in a new season of life and ministry, a newlywed, and I'm trying to figure out what it looks like to invest in women who are younger than me. Sometimes it looks like coffee or brunch with a young woman who just graduated college to talk about life, adulting, and careers. Other times, it's leading a small group of students at church. I have always been one to reach out to other women for advice and wisdom, so I try to make myself available to do the same. Even if it's not your natural inclination, it's a part of being the body of Christ to the women we encounter. No matter what stage of life you're in, you have something to offer a woman younger than you.

HERE ARE A FEW WAYS TO MAKE THIS A PART OF YOUR LIFE ON AN ONGOING BASIS:

- *Be hospitable.* Maybe you don't have time to commit to meeting with someone on a regular basis, but you can open up your home and kitchen table to her. I have a friend who I've learned a ton from just by watching her be a wife and mom. It doesn't have to be formal, but you can take her to run errands with you or have a meal at your table. It's an awesome opportunity to give a college girl a free meal, too. We all remember what it was like to eat ramen noodles in the dorm!

- *Share what you know.* You've been the younger woman, so it's not unfamiliar territory. Share your life experiences and what God has taught you in the process of growing up. She's not looking for an expert, but she is looking for someone to share truth with her.

- *Make yourself available.* Carve out time on your calendar for discipling younger women. It's not easy, but how much time have you spent watching Netflix in the last week? What if just one of those hours (or episodes) was spent intentionally? When I talk to a girl about getting together, I try to put it on the calendar right then so I don't forget.

- *Say "no" when you need to.* There are seasons when you need to let your "no" be someone else's "yes." Give yourself permission to know the season of life you're in, but don't let it become an excuse over time.

- *Pray for opportunities.* Don't take this one lightly. Chances are, if you pray, God will send a younger woman into your life. He'll do it because it matters. We see women in community with other women throughout Scripture, so don't miss the opportunities that may be right in front of you.

- *Don't make it complicated.* It's so easy to overthink things like this and make assumptions. Don't assume other women are too busy or you don't have anything to offer. Just take a chance by saying yes, and see what God does!

Whatever you do, bring it back to Jesus. He is the One we can point girls to, no matter what their season of life looks like at the moment. Share stories of His faithfulness in your life, and be prepared to see Him work in and through the time you give to others.

The whole point of discipleship is this idea of transferring what you know to someone else. Teen girls are desperate for healthy relationships with adults who love Jesus. Many of them have suffered at the hands of adults, or because of the lack of adult presence in their lives. They're longing for someone to show them the way. Will you step up to the plate? Jesus taught and led by example—He didn't pull out a workbook or put people off. He stepped right into their situation and did something about it. Jesus led with His life and let it be the teacher.

Because relational discipleship mattered so much to Jesus, it should deeply matter to us. His life was an incredible example for us to follow, and we have so much we can learn from continuing to understand why Jesus did what He did. There's no doubt Jesus took time for the people He encountered, and they were forever changed as a result. Let's follow the example of Jesus and pray for opportunities to bring girls on the journey.

CHAPTER 2

GET TO KNOW HER

*Part of our job
is to get below the
surface and know the
girls we're loving on
and ministering to.*

Teen girls can be oddly intimidating. I don't know if you've ever walked into a lunchroom full of teenagers, but it's like being back in high school again. I wonder if I'm dressed right, where I'll sit, and what they think of me. It's the craziest thing, but it's been true throughout my student ministry career. We all have an innate need to fit in and find our place, and it doesn't stop when we graduate from high school. On those days, I put my brave face on and look around until I find a student I know. Once we start chatting, the pressure and intimidation begin to fall away.

Have you ever led a small group or Bible study and noticed a girl who looks totally disinterested? That was Alyssa. She was in my eighth grade girls small group one year, and she looked disinterested every week. Every. Week. She would sit in her chair, arms folded across her chest, not participating. Alyssa was difficult to connect with, so I didn't really know what to do. About halfway through the semester, her mom found me on a Sunday morning. She looked at me with a huge smile on her face and said, "Alyssa just LOVES being in your small group on Sundays. She comes home and tells me everything y'all talked about, and I can really see that she's growing!" As I picked my jaw up from the floor, I thanked her and walked away so confused. Alyssa never looked interested. And every week she acted like she didn't even want to be there.

Have you ever met a girl like Alyssa? Funny thing is, I'm really thankful her mom clued me in, or else I might have started to overlook Alyssa. It's much easier to connect with a girl who answers questions, participates, and seems genuinely happy to be there. I'm thankful the Lord gave me a really clear reminder that there are a lot of Alyssas out there. They're in an awkward stage of life that's filled with a ton of transition. They face looming questions on a daily basis and can't figure out where their place is. They want to belong, but they just don't know how. No matter what the situation is with each girl, pray God would allow you to see her the way He sees her. She's in your life for a reason, and you don't want to miss it.

When I got married, I loved opening gifts (I mean, who doesn't love a good place setting or a set of containers with lids?) and reading the notes that came with them. One day, I opened up a gift with a note. Did you already guess who it was from? It was from Alyssa and her mom. I hadn't seen them in years—it's been over ten years since she was in my class. She thanked me for investing in her, and I was brought to tears. I didn't invite them to my wedding, but they wanted to celebrate with me. It's one of the sweetest, most thoughtful gifts I received.

GRACE TO GROW

One of my teacher friends just mentioned a new student in her class and said, "Oh, I've heard through the grapevine that she's going to be difficult." This happens all the time—church, school, jobs, and so on. Put yourself in this girl's shoes for a minute. We're often not able to establish a new version of ourselves because the past version left such a strong mark on other people. As we grow and mature, the Lord can do a powerful work in our hearts and lives. Are we giving girls grace to grow and change, or are we labeling them as difficult, bossy, and annoying?

Some of those bossy, difficult girls have leadership skills welling up within them that someone needs to call out and show them how to use in a healthy way. I was a bossy girl, and if it weren't for the Holy Spirit's role in my life, I would have been a mean girl in high school. I'm glad women stepped into my life at a young age and helped me aim those traits in a more healthy direction.

Scripture reminds us that our words are powerful—they can be life-giving or they can bring death. We've all felt the effects of both of these, but here are some good reminders:

"Death and life are in the power of the tongue..." –Proverbs 18:21a

"The tongue that heals is a tree of life, but a devious tongue breaks the spirit." –Proverbs 15:4

"My dear brothers and sisters, understand this: Everyone should be quick to listen, slow to speak, and slow to anger" –James 1:19

It's much easier to remember the harsh words people have spoken about us than the life-giving ones, so we have to be wise with the way we speak to and about the girls in our life. Take a few minutes and think back to your middle and high school experience.

What do you remember thinking about yourself?

List three things you wish you could tell your middle or high school self.

How can you take those things and share them with girls in your life?

One key thing to remember is not to let the first impression or outward impression be the only thing you rely on. You have to find the avenue that lets you in so you can best minister to girls. Taking this key step will help you figure out why they're doing what they're doing. If you're working hard to figure it out, girls will learn you are trustworthy. They are looking for trustworthy women to help guide them as they grow up and grow in Christ. It's up to you to look below the surface.

New Morning Mercies by Paul David Tripp has become a favorite book of mine. He writes, "We live in long-term networks of terminally casual relationships. No one really knows us beneath the well-crafted public display, and because they don't know us, they cannot minister to us, because no one can minister to that which he does not know."[1] Part of our job is to get below the surface and know the girls we're loving on and ministering to. There are often deep hurts and joys that we miss because we stay on the surface.

Like you read in the introduction, discipleship is going to look somewhat different for each of us, but the key is knowing the girls you're discipling. This won't happen overnight, and it's going to take some intentional effort on your part, but it's well worth it.

If you're discipling a group of girls, every group is going to be different than the next. As you get to know the girls, you'll be able to understand the group dynamic and how you can help the girls engage best. You'll learn things like which girls are verbal processors (me!) and aren't always talking just to talk, but do this to better understand, and which ones aren't going to speak up first because they need some time to think and process. Some girls struggle with insecurities and fears their peers don't, and other girls are coming from really difficult home situations. When you understand the "why" behind what they do, the better you'll be able to understand the girls.

GENERATION Z

Most of you are probably from a different generation than the girls you're discipling. Having an understanding of generational differences can help create pathways for us to have a better understanding of the girls we know and love. If you're anything like me, you probably owned a tape deck at some point in your life (or maybe a record player or eight-track, which basically makes you awesome), remember dial-up Internet, used a green-screen Macintosh at school, and saw the movie Titanic in theaters. You may have had a rotary phone at home, had milk delivered to your front door, and had to walk across the living room to change the TV channel. Girls in Generation Z and after don't know how good we had it!

Girls growing up now are digital natives and have had technology as a part of their entire lives. I've watched some toddlers who can navigate an iPad easier than their parents. The girls in our churches, communities, and lives are online more often than they are in-person. Have you ever watched a group of girls sitting in the same room sending texts or Snapchats to each other? It's easy for a lot of us as adults to say we don't have time to be where they are online, or that we don't want to be on another platform, but we could be missing some opportunities to see what's going on in the lives of girls if we're absent. I talk to leaders all the time who are amazed at what girls will post, knowing their leader will see the video or photo. We don't want to fuel gossip or point fingers, but the door is often wide open to start the conversation. Social media isn't all bad, and we would be wise to be where girls are.

YOUR TURN

To make this work, I'm asking you to write the rest of this chapter. You have a much better pulse on the girls in your church and life than I do, so I don't want you to assume I've got it figured out. Take your time as you answer these questions—there's not a grade for doing this, but it will help you to better evaluate the girls God has put in your life so you can most effectively disciple and minister to them.

Let's first talk about what we see on the surface.

- Define what you see on the surface of the girls in your life.
- What do they look like? (Physical appearance, countenance, dress, style, and so on. Do they try to look older than they are? Do they still act like little girls or do they seem grown up?)
- What can you tell about them without even knowing them well?
- Name a few of the girls you know some surface level things about.
- What's your current involvement with teen girls—is it through your local church? Are you a mom of a teen girl? Are you already discipling or leading a small group?

Now let's go a little deeper and try to identify some things that might not be so obvious.

- What do you already know about the girls in your life that's deeper than the surface?
- What difficult things have gone on in the lives of girls you know within the last year? (parents' divorce, eating disorder, sexual issues, learning disability, death of a loved one, bullying, and so on)

- List a few of the girls you know some deeper level facts about.
- What kinds of questions are they asking about God? Are they even asking spiritual questions?
- Are any of them struggling with ongoing sin issues? What are they?

Now take some time to see what you already know about the girls in your life.

- What are they listening to?
- What are they reading?
- Who do they look up to?
- Who are they following on social media?
- What do they spend their time doing?
- How do they best communicate?
- What are some channels that don't work well when communicating with your girls?

Grab some sticky notes or a journal. On each sticky note or journal page, write out what you know about the girls in your life. Let's aim for positive words, even for girls who feel more difficult to relate to. I've provided a word bank for you if you need some ideas!

- Her name

- What do you already know about her?

- How would you describe her?

- How are you going to pray for her?

WORD BANK

Outgoing	Shy	Quiet	_____
Life of the party	Curious	Eager to learn	_____
Funny	Skeptical	Trusting	_____
Unsure of herself	Serious	Goofy	_____
Reflective	Athletic	Creative	_____
Hardworking	Keeps to herself	Confident	_____

Now that you've evaluated the girl or girls in your life, let's walk through a few more things to keep you thinking.

- What's a next step you can take with the girls you know on a surface level?

- What can you do to take an established friendship further down the road?

- How can you continue to cultivate the relationships you've built with the girls in your life?

- If you're a mom, what do you want to learn about your daughter?

Before we move on to the next chapter, I want to pose a couple of challenges to you.

- Follow them where they are (Instagram, Snapchat, Facebook, and so on). If you don't know how to use it, let them teach you! It's a great way to connect.

- If you don't know some girls very well, try to connect with their parents. This is a great way to earn trust and can shed a lot of light on what's going on when students aren't opening up.

If you don't know a lot about the girls in your life yet, don't be discouraged! This is a great starting point. Over the next few weeks and months, I pray that God will give you opportunities to learn more and build relationships. Don't be afraid to ask and engage, but take your time getting to know them. Show up where they are (sporting events, plays, recitals, and where they work) and let them know you truly care. Even if you've known a girl for a long time, she's in an ever-changing stage of life, so her likes and dislikes may be different than they were last year. Ask God for wisdom as you navigate these friendships, and be obedient to how God would have you walk it out.

Write out a prayer to God for these girls and what you desire for the Lord to do in their lives.

CHAPTER 3

IT'S NOT COMPLI- CATED

If the Lord is putting it on your heart to have a conversation with a young woman, just ask.

We're about to spend the next few pages breaking down discipleship into more manageable pieces. At the heart, it's pretty simple, but it has to be intentional. Now that we've defined discipleship and have a pretty good idea of who the girl or girls are we need to disciple, it's time to get started! One of the biggest questions I get asked about discipleship and mentoring is, "Who is supposed to ask whom?" My response is: if the Lord is putting it on your heart to have a conversation with a young woman, just ask. There's no rhyme, reason, or prescription to it.

I've been on both sides of the coin, and I think either one is effective. Personality types can come into play as to who does the asking, but we would all be wise to pray about it before giving a response.

When I served as a girls minister at a church, I often sought out a handful of girls to meet with on a regular basis for discipleship. My intention was to seek girls who had leadership potential or were in a season where I could tell they needed someone to walk alongside them. The conversations I had with these girls are some of my favorite ministry moments. We walked through accountability questions each week, often memorized Scripture together, and talked about what God was teaching us. I let the girls know on the front end what I expected of them and what they could expect of me, and that made things really clear from the beginning.

One of the most important things you need to remember is you can't do everything other people ask of you. Last year, a girl from church asked me to disciple her, and I had to tell her no. It wasn't because I didn't want to, but because I knew I couldn't commit to what she needed due to commitments I had already made. Before I told her no, I asked what she was looking for when it comes to discipleship. In all honesty, she was really looking for a Bible study partner, so I helped her find a study group. Asking the question of what someone's expectations are is a huge part of being an effective discipler, or deciding that you might not be the right person. Now, before you put this book down and decide you can't commit or you're too busy, ask yourself these questions:

During a regular week, what does my available time look like?

Where are some moments in my schedule when someone could join me in what I'm doing?

Is there something in my life I need to say "no" to, so I can say "yes" to discipling a younger woman?

Now that we've got a baseline about your time, here are some ways I would encourage you:

DISCIPLESHIP ISN'T COMPLICATED

It's so easy to read familiar passages of Scripture without thinking about the context or the implication of what actually happened. I think some of those instances are found early on in the Gospels when Jesus asks the disciples to follow Him. From what we can read, Jesus didn't make a big pitch, and He definitely didn't ask twice. He told them to drop whatever they were doing and follow Him. Jesus knew the urgency of their call. His time was limited, and He was gathering those who would hear, respond, drop everything, and follow Him. He acknowledged what they were doing, and then told them it was time to go.

The first step in being intentional is allowing someone access to you. Go where they are, but also invite them into your life. If you've got a family at home, invite her into your home as you're able. I met Amanda when I was a junior in high school. She was in college and served as an intern in the student ministry at my church that year, and I loved getting to know her and learning from her. Some of my favorite memories with Amanda were driving around in her car singing along to *NSYNC and the Backstreet Boys at the top of our lungs. Amanda would take me alongside her, and that's what discipleship looks like. When I moved to Nashville in 2012, she often invited me over for dinner and let me spend time with her and her family. As a single woman living in a new city, it meant the world to me. They opened their home and lives to me, and I've learned so much from the way they let me be a part of their family. I remember one night in particular when she asked me to come over. Her husband, Bill, was out of town, and I ate dinner with her and their three young kids. We played games, and I helped with bath time, which let her put away the laundry and clean up the house. After the kids went to bed, we sat on the couch and chatted for a couple of hours. We talked about what God was teaching us, and I learned in a very real and practical way what it looks like to be a wife and mom. She invested in me personally by giving me access to herself and her family. Amanda encouraged me in what God was doing in my life, and she has been a woman who has discipled me for more than fifteen years.

I'm so thankful she was willing to let me in. When I was dating Jonathan, my husband, she and her family were some of the first ones to have us over to dinner, and I loved watching Jonathan and Bill get to know each other. Amanda sang two of my favorite songs in my wedding, and I'm beyond thankful for her. While we don't sit at a coffee shop for an hour every week, she disciples me when we're together. I want to learn from her, and she gives me the opportunity to do so on a regular basis.

Many of you may be reading this thinking "no one has ever discipled me—how am I supposed to do this for someone else?" Don't let that be an excuse not to be obedient. Before you totally quit prior to even getting started, answer these questions:

Who are some of the women who have invested in you?

What did they do in your life that made a difference for you?

DISCIPLES ARE READY AND TEACHABLE

One thing we know from reading Scripture is when Jesus asked the men who became His disciples to follow Him, they got up and left whatever they were doing to follow (Matt. 4:19; Mark 1:17; John 1:43). When Jesus prompts us to do something, our call as followers is to obey. We drop what we're doing to follow His instructions. Our comfort is not a valid reason to disobey. This is one of those things we have to be attentive to. God's calling on our lives is specific to us, but He's going to accomplish what He's set out to accomplish whether or not we're on board. The part I love so much is that His desire is to include us in what He's doing to carry out His plans here on earth.

Disciples are ready and teachable. Do you daily surrender yourself to doing whatever God has called you to do that day? Here's the thing—when we ask God to use us, He does. If we aren't asking God to use us, we're flat out missing opportunities. I'm often asked what one leadership tip I would give, and my answer is always the same—stay teachable. If we put ourselves in a posture where we're always willing to learn, it keeps us humble and makes us attentive to what's happening around us.

Jesus asked and the disciples were willing to follow. They left everything behind because Jesus asked them to. Most of you aren't going to be called to go to Africa or Eastern Europe to spend the rest of your life for the sake of the gospel, but some of you will be. The question is—what has He called YOU to do?

What is He asking of you that you're struggling to obey?

Jesus has called us to disciple others—are you going to be obedient?

DISCIPLESHIP BEARS FRUIT

Matthew 7:15-20 speaks plainly about the fact that we'll know people by their fruit, whether it be good fruit or even the bad fruit they produce. What we know to be true is that discipleship bears fruit. When you choose to invest in the life of a teen girl, you will bear fruit and so will she. Talking about the things of God with other believers bears good fruit.

When's the last time you were around a new believer for the weeks and months after she became a Christ follower? It's one of my favorite things to witness and watch because you can see the Holy Spirit actively at work in her life.

She'll share how right before she stepped into sin, something prompted her to stop. The same words don't just roll off her tongue anymore because something has changed. She begins to bear fruit of the One in whom she's put her trust. When we come alongside teen girls and help them see what life in Christ looks like, there's a really good chance things in their lives will change.

DISCIPLESHIP IS REPRODUCIBLE

In our Christian culture today, we have a lot of Christians who are full to overflowing, but they're not pouring into other people. The whole aim of this book is to help you see that what you already know is reproducible in someone else. Teen girls need to know they aren't alone. You can remind them you've been there. They need to hear that life isn't over after high school or college ends. You know—you've experienced it. They may be questioning if God really is who He says He is and wondering if He really is always faithful. You know these things to be true, so tell her. Show her the way. You've been given the knowledge and experiences you have so you can share them with others. Teen girls and young women are ready; they are looking for someone just like you to invest in them. You don't have to be an expert—you just have to be willing.

The book *Simple Student Ministry*, defines discipleship in a way that makes it so clear: "True discipleship is not about information but transformation. Obedience, not knowledge is the bottom line of discipleship ... Discipleship is a process."[1] Just to say it again, discipleship is going to look different for each of us. The process we walk through with each girl or group will have a nuanced feel, and we are simply serving as the guide.

SEVEN KEY ASPECTS OF DISCIPLESHIP

Discipleship happens in a variety of different settings—one on one, small groups, Bible study, and community. In the book *Be a Man*, my friend John Paul Basham established seven key aspects of discipleship that I want to spend the next few pages breaking down for you as it relates to how you can approach discipling teen girls.

1. WOMANHOOD

What it looks like to be a woman is something that feels like a highly charged conversation piece at the moment. What we know to be true is that God designed us to be equal in value, but different in roles than men. I love the fact that I'm a woman. My husband and I process things differently, our emotions are expressed in (what feels like) opposite ways, and our bodies look very different from each other. Rather than spend all of my time tearing apart our differences, I try to be grateful for them. The things that make us different are meant to be celebrated. We're still learning our roles as newlyweds, but we're both embracing the things we're good at and trying to step in where the other is weak. Jonathan leads us well, and I'm very much part of the process.

The Bible gives a beautiful picture of women being a helpmate, not a doormat. There's a huge difference, and we need to know what the difference is. While you may not get into a long conversation with a girl on womanhood and the roles of women, you need to help girls realize that God created them uniquely and on purpose. Womanhood is something that makes them who they are, and it's something they can embrace. This doesn't in any way mean they have to wear makeup, love to dress up, or wear glittery shoes. (Not that there's anything wrong with glittery shoes.) It does mean we are key players in God's plan for His kingdom here on earth, and He created us on purpose.

2. THEOLOGY

You don't have to be a theologian to love and follow Jesus, but you do need to be in an ongoing pursuit of understanding who God is because "theology informs our thinking, shapes our feelings, instructs our living, and when engaged humbly, moves us to worship."[2] If you don't have a seminary degree, don't freak out. This idea of growing in theology can be really intimidating, but it's not meant to be. The fact of the matter is we're never going to have it all figured out, but we should be on a constant quest to learn and grow as followers of Christ. When we better understand who He is and why the Bible matters so much, it changes the way we live. It will also change the way you disciple girls. If you commit to being a lifelong learner, you'll always be growing. This is a great opportunity to ask the student pastor at your church, your senior pastor, or other friends in ministry for help. If you don't already know what your church believes and why, ask. Be knowledgeable so you can share that knowledge with others.

3. SPIRITUAL DISCIPLINES

I could write a whole book on this, but there are a few experts out there who have already done a great job. Spiritual disciplines often feel unapproachable or like something we can't understand, so we just avoid learning about them. I've had the opportunity to write blog posts on how to read the Bible, why it's important to memorize Scripture, and what the Bible says about fasting. They have been some of my favorite things to dive into, and as we help girls understand what it looks like to follow Jesus, these practices are a huge part of the process.

When is the last time you examined spiritual disciplines in your own life?

If you don't feel like you have a good grip on these, hang on because we're going to talk about them in detail a little later.

4. PERSONAL HOLINESS

A book I've loved for a long time is *The Pursuit of Holiness* by Jerry Bridges. This is actually a book I went through as a high school student when I was being discipled by my student pastor's wife, so it's near and dear to my heart. As followers of Christ, we are called to be holy. Scripture tells us in 1 Peter 1:16, "Be holy, because I am holy." Holiness is an ongoing pursuit for the duration of our lives. Discipleship will produce holiness—it's a natural by-product of the process. The world will try to do everything it can to distract girls from what they were created to do, but the more girls pursue holiness, the clearer the lines are and their focus is where it needs to be. Sin and the enemy are very real threats, but a lifelong pursuit of holiness is a way to stand up against his schemes.

5. MISSION

We are all called to be ministers of the gospel. It's easy to think that the only people who are missionaries are those who are called to live overseas, but we have opportunities each day to be missional in the way we live our lives. Paul reminds us in Galatians 2:20, "I have been crucified with Christ, and I no longer live, but Christ lives in me. The life I now live in the body, I live by faith in the Son of God, who loved me and gave himself for me." We need to remember Christ's sacrifice and share the truth of the gospel with others who do not yet know Him.

6. LEADERSHIP

Discipleship is leadership. We see how Titus 2 gives women the charge to teach and encourage younger women, and this includes equipping them to lead. As believers, leadership is always Christ-centered, and when we lead well, we have an incredible opportunity to make an impact on others. We often miss the chance to help bossy, strong-willed girls see how God can use these things to make them strong leaders. As we disciple girls, we must help them see how God can use them to lead wherever He calls them.

7. DISCIPLE MAKING

I hope this one is pretty obvious by this point—discipleship is mandatory and critical. I love how John Paul states, "Jesus took ordinary men and transformed them into world changers. Jesus' first disciples were fishermen, tax collectors, and political activists when He called them. When they died, they had become pastors, church planters, and martyrs. These men not only followed Jesus passionately, but they also multiplied themselves. They embraced Jesus' call to make disciples of all nations."[3] The call to make disciples is clear. Will you obey?

CALLED TO DISCIPLE

One of my best friends works with college girls through the avenue of Baptist Collegiate Ministry. She has a clear call on her life, and I love hearing stories of how God is moving among the girls she disciples. I asked Corley Shumaker to share with you why the call to disciple teen girls is so crucial, and how it impacts them after high school graduation.

CORLEY'S STORY

As someone who has worked with college students on a daily basis for the last thirteen years, the ones who stand out are the ones who have experienced real discipleship before they come to college. When they come in with a background of discipleship, they're far more prepared for what college is going to throw at them. They have the resources to deal with hardships. They know how to seek out godly counsel, and they don't balk when someone holds their feet to the fire of accountability.

If we don't disciple our girls, how are they going to learn what it means to be a woman of God at twenty-five, fifty, or seventy-five? How will they know that they can stick it out in high school, singleness, marriage, parenthood, widowhood, and every other season of life unless we live it in front of them? They must see us navigating the good and the bad, and occasionally they even need to see us handle it poorly, but still come out of it choosing Jesus. They must see us refusing to give up.

Discipleship in my teen years made a huge difference in my life during college and beyond. The women who were consistently there and who loved me through teenage drama provided stability I desperately needed in the uncertain world of high school. They prayed over me, invested in me, and believed in me. They gave me leadership opportunities. When I blew it, they turned those situations into teaching moments. Even when I wasn't necessarily meeting with them one-on-one for focused discipleship, their presence provided boundaries. I knew their eyes were on me, and I wanted to make them proud. Their influence in my life during high school caused me to seek out similar influences in college. There has never been a season of my life since then when I have not sought out the friendship and counsel of an older woman.

Discipleship can be as theologically deep as you want it to be, but for me it's as simple as extending my hand to someone younger than me and saying, "I know this life of faith is hard, but Jesus is worth it." How do I know? Because someone said the same thing to me, either with their words or by how they lived their life, and as I have walked with the Lord, I have found it to be true.

You aren't solely responsible for the spiritual health of every teen girl you know, but you are responsible to do what you can with what you know. Some girls you spend years investing in will graduate college and completely walk away from their faith. This can be devastating and really hard to understand, but you have to trust that you have planted and watered spiritual seeds in their life that God can use. Some of the girls you pour into are going to flourish and grow in ways you never imagined. That part isn't up to you—it's what only the Holy Spirit can do in the lives of girls. Be faithful with the time you have, and be intentional with your life. You won't regret it.

CHAPTER 4

WHY ME?

As followers of Christ, we are all called to be ministers of the gospel.

As I'm sitting here today writing, I'm thinking about you. Most days, I don't feel qualified to do much of anything, much less be writing a book that's now printed and in your hands. But if I didn't write this, I would have been disobedient. There's a really good chance you feel inadequate to do what God has called you to do. Let me encourage you that you have everything you need if you have Jesus. If you know Him and are walking with Him, you're adequate for the task at hand. I love in Exodus 4 when Moses lists every reason he's not the right one for the job. If you'll look back at Exodus 3, this happens right after God speaks to Moses through a burning bush. Like a literal bush on fire. A talking, burning bush isn't enough for Moses. Really?

Sometimes it's as if we're waiting on a burning bush when God has already given us clear instructions. We are begging God to write it in the sky, light it on fire, and give us the most obvious sign possible, and He already has. What are we waiting for? Today, I'm challenging you to take the next step.

Is there something you've been hesitating to do? If you don't do it, would it be an act of disobedience?

Whatever God has called you to do, do it. Do it without hesitation. Don't second-guess God. If He calls you to it, He will give you what you need.

What's the next step you can take today?

This morning, I was reading out of John 6 where Jesus explains that He is the Bread of life. He tells the disciples and those listening that He is the only thing that will sustain them. Anything other than Him will not last. We are so easily convinced that the things of this world will bring us life, when in all reality, many of them are life-draining.

Maybe you're not questioning your leadership abilities or willingness to disciple a group of girls. When was the last time you gave yourself a heart check to make sure you're serving in the right place in the current season you're in?

> **Examine your heart and ask God where He might have you serve that you might have previously not considered or may have even avoided.**

GOD SAYS

Let's look at some passages of Scripture that speak to what God says about us:

In Christ, you are set free. –John 8:36

In Christ, you are loved. –1 John 4:10

In Christ, you are forgiven. –Psalm 32:1

In Christ, you are more than a conqueror. –Romans 8:37

In Christ, you are a daughter of the Most High. –John 1:12

When we aren't spending time with Jesus, we become empty. Maybe you're still trying to feed off of a sermon you heard six months ago, hoping that it will still give you life. That might be a good reminder, but what fresh and new thing are you learning? If you're not regularly being fed and drinking from the well of Living Water, you won't have much to offer to girls, or anyone else for that matter.

Your obedience matters. Just because you're serving and leading doesn't mean you're being wholeheartedly obedient. Jesus calls us to be obedient in every area of our lives. He desires for us to walk closely with Him, and for some of us, it means some things in our lives need to change.

What does your time with God look like?

If you don't feel like you're in a great place spiritually, what are some changes you can make?

Is anyone investing in you? If so, who? If not, have you prayed that God would send someone to invest in you?

DEPEND ON GOD

If you know you are called but struggle to shake those feelings of inadequacy, one way I would encourage you is to allow those feelings to help you lead with humility. If you've walked closely with Jesus for a long time, lead with humility. If you're a newer follower of Jesus or you've just come out of a really hard season of life, lead with humility. God can do a ton with a heart that is humble before Him. When we feel like we've got it all together, we make it hard to hear from

God because we're basically telling Him we've got it figured out all on our own. Dependence on Him is crucial when we lead.

At this point in my life, it's really easy for me to discern when I'm working and serving out of my flesh or out of my dependence on God. I've finished teaching a conference session to sit down and realize I was too dependent on myself. I didn't fully surrender, and I knew it. While God can still use that, it's not a position you want to put yourself in. When I know that I couldn't have done it without Him, I know it wasn't me.

Even as I'm writing this, I'm begging God to give me wisdom and insight as I try to convey this message He has put on my heart. I've had to erase paragraph after paragraph that sounded like "good thoughts from Mary Margaret" and replace them with paragraphs that hopefully don't make much of me.

I think of Acts 4 when Peter and John are before the Jewish Council. These disciples were boldly proclaiming the truth of Jesus, and they were then questioned about what they believed by the religious rulers. They were arrested and put before the council to answer questions about Jesus. When they took a stand for what they believed, the council was astonished. They responded by saying, "When they observed the boldness of Peter and John and realized that they were uneducated and untrained men, they were amazed and recognized that they had been with Jesus" (Acts 4:13).

Here's the deal—Peter and John were untrained, common men. They weren't great communicators, they didn't have seminary degrees, and this isn't what they had spent their lives doing. They believed so strongly in Jesus that they couldn't help but talk about Him. Peter and John wanted everyone to know the man who had radically changed their lives, so they were unashamed to share about Him.

Is anything holding you back from living boldly for Jesus, so the girls in your life can see?

Can the girls in your life tell that you spend time with Jesus?

There's so much power in being able to share with someone else what you learned in Scripture that day. By spending time in God's Word, you are prepared for whatever you may face that day. You're more apt to speak His truth and wisdom than on your own. You're more in tune with the Holy Spirit. You're prayed up and ready to go for whatever comes your way that day.

A PICTURE OF DISCIPLESHIP

My friend Amy Burgess has been a discipler of young women for as long as I've known her, and she started discipling me and several of my friends while we were in high school. I want you to hear some perspective from both sides of discipleship—both from Amy's perspective as the discipler and from my friend Jessica Staton's perspective, as the one being discipled.

JESSICA'S STORY:

Yma. An affectionate (and strange) nickname for the single most influential person in my life aside from my parents. Her actual name is Amy. I remember meeting her at camp between my sophomore and junior years of high school. Amy, with her volume-all-the-way-up bullhorn, was my cabin counselor. She was intense, loud, and had a big smile and a matter-of-fact personality. There was something about Amy that made my spirit say, "Yes!" I wanted what she had and that was a whole lot of Jesus.

I had a year of Sunday school with Amy and felt like there was more there for me. So a couple of girls from our youth group and I asked Amy if she would meet with us outside of our regular Sunday time—to teach us to pray, and in hindsight, how to live like Jesus. We wanted to be discipled! And we saw in Amy something we wanted to emulate.

Exactly what we did for those eighty or so minutes didn't make as much of an impact on me as just living my life with Amy and her family. Her husband and two young children (at the time) were as much a part of that discipleship experience. I occasionally babysat for their children, but I always just wanted to be around—to play with her kids, to go on trips to Clemson football games with them, to help shuttle her kids to football, and just share in the rhythms of life. I saw how Amy and her husband Rob lived, how they loved and raised their kids. We talked about any and everything. No subjects were off limits, and I knew that relationship was always a safe landing place for me when my heart was broken or if I was mad at my parents. She and Rob encouraged me to see my life through the lens of Jesus. Not too self-righteous or holier than thou—but REAL. To live like Jesus mattered to me and the decisions I made in my life, big and small, reflected that.

I am so much older now and have a husband and family of my own, and I still so often reference those years I spent (in high school and college) living alongside their family. I feel it needs to be said that it speaks to their family and to the pursuit of discipleship. But now I see that it was also God's unspeakable love and tender provision for me. I have known a depth of God's love through my discipleship journey that I am certain I would not have known on my own. Not only did I have Amy and her precious family cheering me on, but the Lord was drawing me ever closer to Himself—preparing me for the life I have now and the ministry and family challenges I have faced.

AMY'S STORY:

What I grew up calling discipleship and what I think discipleship is now, at the age of forty-eight, are close to complete opposites. When I was in seventh grade, I was discipled by my youth pastor. It was a once a week meeting in a small group setting where we checked off boxes about how many times we had prayed and read our Bibles that week, memorized a verse, and studied some Scripture. I memorized my first Scripture passage and loved learning about the Bible, so as I grew up and was able to disciple younger people, I generally followed this pattern. Although there is nothing biblically incorrect with any of the things we did in discipleship, as I have grown older, Jesus has given me a clearer picture of His less "churchy" and generally more costly view of what the Bible really means when it tells us to go and make disciples.

The Bible verse that best describes how I believe Christ discipled His own disciples is 1 Thessalonians 2:7b-8:

> Instead we were gentle among you, as a nurse nurtures her own children. We cared so much for you that we were pleased to share with you not only the gospel of God but also our own lives, because you had become dear to us.

This is how I believe He wants us to disciple others. Not that a weekly commitment and some Bible study are wrong—they just aren't enough. In this verse the people doing the discipling are humble. They care about all the needs—physical, emotional, spiritual, and so on—of the one God has given them to teach and learn from! They are motivated by genuine, real Christlike sacrificial love. True discipleship, just like in the Bible, is going to get messy and ugly because real relationships involve real sinners.

Being a relational person by nature, I spent my college summers interning with my youth group and becoming a small group leader to groups of younger girls. This was the beginning of a lifetime of discipleship. Years later, a speaker at a women's event encouraged me to use any home God gave me to practice hospitality, regardless of its size or beauty. These two pieces of advice merged and changed my view of what discipling someone entailed as I grew up, got married, and bought homes.

You see, real discipleship for me has often involved God first inserting a person into my life who had a need. Often the need was for a place to live or the ability to earn money. I could provide these things, and they in turn provided me with the help I needed at the time. True discipleship always comes with a cost to everyone.

However, it is a cost that is negligible compared to the spiritual rewards Christ brings as a result.

When I give all that God has given me back to Him and I refresh others, I will be refreshed (Prov. 11:25). As I have opened my homes throughout the seasons of my life, the small unfurnished ones as well as the spacious and nicely decorated ones, God has brought these people into my life to pour into physically, financially, emotionally, and then spiritually, usually in that order. I didn't choose them or necessarily even pray for them. He just brought them, and I just opened the door.

As we refresh others with the things God has blessed us with, including our families and our homes, our bank accounts and our time, we (and in my experience, our children too) will be refreshed. A few times we have had people live with us for a short period of time. Many times we have had people share our home and our family on holidays or other family times. This has always blessed us and our children, even for years after. It has taught us to live like we say we believe. The people in our home who we are discipling see the real-life stuff. We want to be real, and we also want our "real" to still glorify God and match what we preach. That often means apologizing for the real because we know it's not always right. It has taught us to be unselfish. It is a constant reminder that our home is Jesus' home, not ours. It has blessed us to have people there to not only help us with our children, but to influence our children for Christ. It has taught our children that although family is important, it is not to be idolized or exclusive. Christ says to love our neighbors as ourselves, and our enemies more. Over many years, the Lord has brought far greater spiritual and physical rewards to me and my family members than any cost that was ever involved in me discipling someone. I have also been blessed with a few spiritual children and grandchildren over the last twenty-five years as a result. Jessica and her family are some of these.

Jesus opened up His life for others and commands us to do the same. There are others who will bless us, as has been my general experience, as well as those who may betray us, which has also happened a time or two. Allowing myself and my family to experience this type of discipleship is way beyond *what my original small group, box-checking idea of the term allowed for, and yet, Jesus commands us to do it. He commands us to first serve, care for, and give our lives to those He brings us before we start teaching and instructing.*

WALK OUT YOUR CALLING

We toss around a lot of conversation on the topic of "What am I called to do?" and it can be a really confusing place to be. To give calling a definition, let's say it's where we become fully alive and awake to what God has put us here to do. There are things He's going to call us to for the rest of our lives, and things He's going to call us to for a season. Let's explore what it looks like to walk out our calling when it comes to discipleship.

The Letter of 2 Timothy provides a great framework for us to use as we dive in. At this point in their lives and ministry, Paul and Timothy had known each other for about twenty years, and Paul was writing this letter from prison. This was Paul's last letter in Scripture, and the second letter written specifically to Timothy. In the second verse he says, "To Timothy, my dearly loved son" (2 Tim. 1:2). They are like a father and son in the faith, and Paul has invested much of his life into Timothy.

Paul poses a challenge to Timothy and says:

> *"I thank God, whom I serve with a clear conscience as my ancestors did, when I constantly remember you in my prayers night and day. Remembering your tears, I long to see you so that I may be filled with joy. I recall your sincere faith that first lived in your grandmother Lois and in your mother Eunice and now, I am convinced, is in you also. Therefore, I remind you to rekindle the gift of God that is in you through the laying on of my hands. For God has not given us a spirit of fear, but one of power, love, and sound judgment."* –2 Timothy 1:3-7

One of the things I love about this passage is that it shows women were the ones who taught Timothy about Jesus. His grandmother Lois and his mother Eunice were both followers of Jesus, and they taught Timothy what they knew. These women left a godly heritage behind, and Timothy was pivotal in the spread of the gospel as a result of their faithfulness.

In this passage, Paul encourages Timothy to do something with what he taught him. Paul was aware that he's sitting in prison, and his days were numbered. He used the words "remember" and "remind" several times in the passage because he's thinking back, but also to make sure that Timothy knows these things and doesn't forget.

Why is it important to walk out the calling God has placed on your life? We all have unique callings. Every single one of you who's reading this is going to disciple a teen girl in a different way. The goal is the same, but the method is personal to you. Only you can fulfill the unique calling God has placed on your life. Paul writes in Colossians 3:23, "Whatever you do, do it from the heart, as something done for the Lord and not for people ..." He is charging us to do whatever we do with great excellence because it's for the Lord, not for other people.

When we get frustrated at church or with the people we serve, it's easy to start serving halfway. We're frustrated, so we quit giving 100 percent. This gets you nowhere, friend. Our job is to hold our heads high and serve as unto the Lord. Some of my hardest ministry days were working with other people in ministry. Serving the local church by being on staff has truly been one of the greatest joys of my life, but sometimes it's really hard because you're sinful and sometimes crazy, and you're working with people who are sinful and sometimes crazy. There were definitely days I wanted to throw in the towel, but God called me (and calls all of us) to serve as unto *Him* alone.

Discipleship is something we've all been called to. Matthew 28 is probably a familiar passage. Jesus had just been resurrected from the dead and was making Himself known to the disciples and others who were around. His last recorded words before He ascended into heaven were, "All authority has been given to me in heaven and on earth. Go, therefore, and make disciples of all nations ..." (Matt. 28:18-19). Going and making disciples isn't optional. Part of being faithful in our calling is walking it out in a way that's worthy of what we've been called to. Paul reminds believers in Ephesians 4:1-6 that we are to walk worthy of what we've been called to do.

Can we also just clear one thing up? A call to vocational ministry isn't a greater calling than any other calling—it's just a different one. As followers of Christ, we are all called to be ministers of the gospel. Some people are called to serve in a full-time job in ministry, but most of us aren't. We're called to be ministers of the gospel in hair salons, classrooms, operating rooms, boutiques, and certainly in our homes. If you're frustrated that your paycheck and your calling aren't tied together, you may stay frustrated. Not all of us are going to be paid to do the thing we are called to do.

DON'T MISS OUT

When I was a seminary student, I always felt broke. I had already been serving in full-time ministry, but when I made the decision to follow God's call on my life to pursue a master's degree in seminary, I quit my full-time job and took a part-time job. I'll never forget what it felt like to stand at the gas pump and watch each hour of hard work go into my gas tank or to ring up groceries and see where my hard-earned money was going in a way I'd never experienced before. My last year of seminary, I was getting ready to head home for Thanksgiving and Christmas, and realized my car needed an oil change before I made the drive from New Orleans, Louisiana to Little Rock, Arkansas, where my parents were living at the time. I didn't have the money to get an oil change, so I prayed that somehow God would provide an oil change for me. It honestly was the most awkward prayer I've ever prayed because who prays for an oil change? I wasn't sure what was going to happen, but I knew I needed to give it over to the Lord.

A few days later, my friend Wanda who worked on campus at the seminary sent me a Facebook message: "Mary Margaret, where do you get your oil changed? A little bird asked me and I did not have a clue how to find out. Aunt Jo Ann wants to give you an oil change for Christmas! Please don't let on that I asked!!" This happened seven years ago, and it still brings tears to my eyes every time I tell the story. Wanda has worked at the seminary for decades and knew my Great Aunt Jo Ann Leavell, so she was trying to help her out with this Christmas gift.

Here's the deal—this story isn't about the fact that I got what I prayed for. This story is about the fact that my Great Aunt, who lived 650 miles away from me, knew God was calling her to give me an oil change for Christmas, so she did it. She obeyed. She was faithful to the thing God had called her to do, even though it probably sounded weird at the time. Can I also take a second to mention that every year for Christmas before and after this, she gave me twenty dollars in five dollar bills? That one year, she gave me (and all of my cousins) oil changes.

When we miss out on doing the thing God calls us to do, will He still accomplish His purpose? Absolutely. But when we miss out, we might rob other people of the chance to see God's hand at work. Could God have provided an oil change another way? Yes. But He chose to use my Aunt Jo Ann, and she chose to be obedient. Her faithfulness still moves me, and I don't ever want to miss an opportunity to be the hands and feet of Jesus to the people around me because it might sound weird or different.

Are you worried that saying yes to God might look weird to the people around you?

Can you think of an example of when God has used your obedience to impact someone else?

I'm not sure I ever told my Aunt Jo Ann how much that oil change meant to me before she passed away. Her obedience has been a living testimony to me, and I wish I had told her.

I'm going to ask you to do something. If I was sitting across the table from you, I'd be able to be a little bit more persuasive, so just pretend that's the case. I want you to take a few minutes right now (or maybe even a couple of days) to ask God to clarify your calling.

Here's what we already know:

- He's called you to be a minister of the gospel.
- He's called you to disciple.

With those two tasks at hand, ask Him what this needs to look like in your life. Ask Him to open your eyes to see the women and girls around you who need someone to step up to the plate and disciple them. Maybe it's the teen daughter in your own house. It might be a girl in the small group you lead. It could be a girl you haven't even met yet, but she's coming your way soon. Is God calling you to launch a girls ministry in your local church? Read back over some of the passages of Scripture we've covered in this chapter, and ask God to show you the way so you can show *her* the way.

What are you going to do with what you know?

What do you believe God has called you to do when it comes to discipling teen girls?

What are you afraid of?

Don't be discouraged when other people question your calling. My dad has been in ministry his whole life and career, and I've loved hearing his stories and meeting people who would call my dad a spiritual hero. It's a huge blessing to be J.B. Collingsworth's daughter. When I first felt a calling on my life to work in ministry, my dad had a hard time seeing where the idea of girls ministry fit into the picture, because it wasn't something he'd seen in his 20 plus years of student ministry. I had to explain to him that it wasn't a separate ministry in the church, but a way to allow women to come alongside teen girls in an intentional way through the local church. (I'm sure I couldn't explain it quite like this when I was twenty-one, but track with me here.) I knew I was called to pour into the next generation of women, but even my own dad was hesitant at first. Now he's one of my biggest cheerleaders in ministry, and he has been for years.

I want to challenge you to tell someone what God is calling you to do. Sometimes verbalizing it can be both the hardest and most freeing part. Ask one of your girlfriends to hold you accountable to walk this out, even when it gets hard. Discouragement will crop up, girls will be feisty and difficult, and you're going to want to quit. When you want to give up, you need someone who can hold your feet to the fire. I've got a tight circle of friends that are these kind of women in my life. If you don't have that, I'm praying God would provide that kind of friend for you. We all need other women in our corner praying for us! Whatever you do, don't miss the opportunity to be used by God in a way that only you can. He doesn't need us, but He certainly loves to use us to bring glory to His name.

CHAPTER 5

SETTING OUT

You don't have to have all of the answers—you just have to be willing.

If I'm being completely honest with you, I'm a pretty selfish person. I'm selfish with my time probably more than anything else, but in general, I could be described as a selfish woman. (Mom, I know you're reading this and taught me better. I'm sorry.)

Now that we've gotten true confessions out of the way, let me tell you it's something I'm actively working on. Awhile back, my pastor preached a sermon series called "The Best is Yet to Come," and he asked us to write down three things we want other people to be able to say about us. Number three on my list says, "Her time is not her own—she is available and pursues time with others." Our church staff collected these cards and then mailed them to us at the end of the summer, and I've been amazed at how God has stretched me in these three areas, but especially in the area of my time and how I spend it. I've taped the card to my mirror, so I see it every day and am reminded of the importance of making time for others.

- It's because of the card on my mirror that I volunteered to serve in the nursery at church when they needed volunteers.
- It's because of the card on my mirror that I talked to a younger woman about discipling her.
- It's because of the card on my mirror that I turned the TV off to have a conversation with a friend.

At the end of my life, I want people to say I made time for them, and I sacrificed for the sake of others. No one is going to be crying over the fact that I knew everything about this season's "Dancing with the Stars" when my life is over. I want my time to have mattered.

PERSPECTIVE SHIFT

When we look at the Letters of 1 & 2 Timothy, we see Paul's relationship with Timothy and the personal nature of the letters. We know from history that this relationship wasn't brand new—it was well-established and had taken place over the course of about 20 years. Paul writes in a personal way to Timothy because he knew him. These two men had walked through a season of life together, and it's obvious. This came about because Paul made time and Timothy was willing. When Paul writes to Timothy about the godlessness that is coming in the last days, he says, "For people will be lovers of self, lovers of money, boastful, proud ..." (2 Tim. 3:2). Being a lover of self is considered godlessness. Ouch. This is a huge call for us to make a change. He's admonishing Timothy, and there's a lot we can learn from this challenge.

Shifting your perspective to focus more on others comes at a cost. It's going to cost you things like time, money, and energy. It means something is going to get put on the back burner. It's causing me to think ahead and make decisions that aren't just about today and right now. Our culture demands instant gratification, but God doesn't work that way. Relationships aren't forged overnight, and cultivating them simply takes time.

As you look at the next few months, what changes could you make to focus less on yourself?

What are some ways God is prompting you to focus more on others?

Our call as Christ followers is to steward well the time and resources we have. Maybe it's time to make a list of things you want others to say about you. Today is a great day to start.

It's time to start the conversation with the girl or girls you've been praying about discipling. Set up a time to get together and talk, and see what happens! One of the best things you can do is have a clear understanding of your purposes and expectations. You want to be able to clearly communicate this to both the girls and their parents, and know what your church policies are as well if any of this is through your church.

As you dive into discipleship, remember that you're not the hero in this story—Jesus is. You don't have to have all of the answers; you just have to be willing.

A story that has become one of my favorites over the last few years is from Acts 8—it's the story of Philip and the Ethiopian eunuch. Let's read Acts 8:26-29.

> *An angel of the Lord spoke to Philip: "Get up and go south to the road that goes down from Jerusalem to Gaza." (This is the desert road.) So he got up and went. There was an Ethiopian man, a eunuch and high official of Candace, queen of the Ethiopians, who was in charge of her entire treasury. He had come to worship in Jerusalem and was sitting in his chariot on his way home, reading the prophet Isaiah aloud. The Spirit told Philip, "Go and join that chariot."*

List two significant things that stand out to you in this passage.

What can we learn from Philip in this story?

There are girls out there who are waiting on someone to step up and walk with them. They're trying to understand, and they just need a guide. Will you be the one? Will you show her the way? Philip was obedient to follow what the angel of the Lord said, and he dropped everything to follow the instructions. He had no idea what he was getting himself into, but he wasn't going to be disobedient. When the Spirit gave Philip more specific instructions, he again obeyed. My favorite part of the passage says this (vv. 30-31):

> "When Philip ran up to [the chariot], he heard him reading the prophet Isaiah, and said, "Do you understand what you're reading?" "How can I," he said, "unless someone guides me?"

Friends, you are the guide. Younger girls and women need you to guide them and point them to truth. None of us were meant to do this alone. There's no way any of us will ever fully understand everything, so we have to help each other. You don't have to have all of the answers—you just have to be obedient. I'm going to share some ways throughout this chapter that you can get started. If you feel like you're already doing some of this, let it be an encouragement that you're on the right track!

PRAY AND BE IN THE WORD DAILY

This is so straightforward, but can be really difficult in some seasons. I'm admittedly not the most disciplined person I know. I'm a night owl, I love hitting the snooze button, and I'm usually running a few minutes late in the morning no matter how much time I give myself. All of these things have been excuses for me in one season or another as to why I can't spend time with God in the morning. Different times of day work better in different seasons, but right now, mornings work best, so that's why I try to make it happen then. This step of daily obedience is a critical one for all of us. How can we lead if we aren't daily ready for battle? What insight and wisdom do we have to share if we haven't asked God for it that day? These questions are the gut-punch kind. None of this is said to make you feel shame or guilt—it's just to remind us that the only one who determines your priorities is you. If I stay up too late watching a show on Netflix, it's on me. There's no one else to blame here.

I'll be perfectly honest and tell you I've gotten into seasons (even recently) when spending time with the Lord is hard. Sometimes it's because of my lack of discipline, but other times it's because I'm trying to control too much. When I get too controlling and want to be in charge of my life for a hot second, God quickly reminds me that I'm not in charge of much of anything.

When we spend time with God, we're not only setting ourselves up to know Him more, we're setting an example for other believers, especially the girls and young women we're discipling.

LEARN FROM LEADERS

While I was in seminary, I had the privilege of working alongside Dr. Allen Jackson. At the time, he taught the youth ministry classes, and I served as his assistant and grader for a year. In his book *TEACH: The Ordinary Person's Guide to Teaching Students the Bible,* he writes:

> *"Learning and transformation happen through relationships between youth ministers and adults, adults and students, students and youth ministers, and so on. We learn in relationships. We believe the Bible has information that is both life- and eternity-changing. Therefore, half of the equation is building relationships and the other half is sharing—as well as we possibly can—the story of God's great love and redemptive purpose for humankind."[1]*

Dr. Jackson taught me so much about building relationships, and I'll forever be thankful he did. As his assistant, I got to know most of his students, and I'm not sure any professor on campus had more students in their office than Dr. Jackson. He masterfully built relationships with students, even the not-so-easy-to-love ones. His students were more engaged in class and in their work because they knew he was the real deal. He set an example for those of us who were there to learn, and it went far beyond the classroom. He and his wife, Judi, hosted all of the youth ministry students in their home, he helped repair my car and change my oil on a number of occasions (as well as countless other students), and he took the time to listen and help any student who needed his time. These are the kinds of leaders we would be wise to learn from.

BE INVOLVED IN STUDENT MINISTRY

So much of the growth I've experienced spiritually has come as a result of being involved in student ministry in the local church. It's come from my experiences in sixth to twelfth grades, but it's also from my experiences serving and teaching. Teens have a propensity to ask really challenging questions, and I've had to do a lot of digging and asking over the years to help them better understand the Bible, which has helped me to better understand the Bible. The better I knew students personally, the more freely they asked the questions on their hearts and minds. I've had the incredible privilege of learning from some of the absolute best servant leaders and student pastors on the face of the earth. My student pastors and friends taught me more about leading by doing than anyone else. I'm grateful for their lives and impact, and I wouldn't be who I am today without their influence.

ESTABLISH A GIRLS MINISTRY

If your church doesn't have a specific ministry for teen girls, have you ever thought that it might be you who can step up and lead? This is a great way to gain some support and structure for discipleship. A lot of student pastors would *love* for a woman to come alongside and pour into the lives of the girls in their ministry. Connecting with other small group or Sunday school teachers and being involved in the events your student ministry is putting on can provide incredible pathways for discipleship to start.

I've had the privilege of helping to establish a girls ministry in a couple of churches, as well as walking with other women through this process. My first question would be this:

What's your aim in starting a girls ministry?

Girls ministry isn't necessarily about establishing a program that has a budget, theme, and a T-shirt. It's a targeted way to intentionally minister to the needs of teen girls through the local church. It takes women who are ready to share their lives with girls and invest their time in girls, and it doesn't have to be complicated. There's not a "one size fits all" way to start girls ministry, but some of you are going to have the incredible privilege of leading out in this way. Some of you are going to find yourselves in a job leading a girls ministry, and some of you are going to lead it as a volunteer. Both of these are incredibly important! The goal is to help girls find their place in your church and come alongside to minister to their needs.

Some of my favorite girls ministry moments come from parties, worship nights, and fashion shows, but not just because we had fun—we shared the gospel with girls who came and saw God move in powerful ways. You can have a ton of fun and still be purposeful and intentional with whatever you plan. If you haven't noticed, teen girls are a lot like women. They're just the younger version! They like to do things with other girls, be in community together, and will often open up much more than when in mixed gender groups.

Girls ministry has been a clear calling on my life for almost fifteen years. While it's looked different depending on the seasons of my life and the churches I've served, I've always had younger women in my life I can pour into, most of whom have come through my local church.

IF YOU'RE STRUGGLING WITH HOW TO TALK TO YOUR STUDENT PASTOR ABOUT STARTING A GIRLS MINISTRY, HERE ARE FIVE WAYS TO BEGIN THE CONVERSATION:

1. *Share the calling God has placed on your life to disciple and minister to girls.*

2. *Ask if and how you can come alongside what he is already doing to start intentional groups, events, and strategies specifically to reach the girls in your church and community.*

3. *Make a list of creative ways to engage girls and share your ideas with him.*

4. *Think about it from his perspective—there's probably a lot already in the works, on the calendar, and budget money has been allocated. This is where you can be creative, but also sometimes patient.*

5. *Give him some time to think and pray about what God could do through girls ministry in your church. Don't assume you'll get a "yes" from your first conversation.*

WHAT NOT TO DO WHEN IT COMES TO TALKING TO YOUR STUDENT PASTOR ABOUT GIRLS MINISTRY:

1. *Don't tell him what you're going to do. Share your heart and ideas and lead well.*

2. *Don't say that he's not effectively reaching girls, and you've come to save the day and do the job. He's the one with the role, so respect his position in your church.*

3. *Don't talk in paragraphs. Give bullet point ideas that are straightforward and to the point.*

4. *Don't go behind his back and talk to his boss. Follow the proper chain of command.*

5. *Don't assume that "no" means never—it could just mean not right now. Continue to pray and seek God's direction.*

Girls need good, godly male examples in their lives. Your student pastor is very likely one of these men, so affirm what he does well! Girls ministry shouldn't downplay the role of a student pastor in the life of students, but should complement what's already happening in your church.

SEEK TRAINING & DEVELOPMENT OPPORTUNITIES

There are more and more opportunities for your own personal training and development as you begin to disciple girls. Whether it's a leadership conference, podcasts, blogs, or other books and resources, there are countless tools out there at your disposal. Grab one of your friends and find some leadership training and conferences that you can attend together.

In Acts 5, we find Peter and John before the council. They're defending their beliefs in front of religious leaders and are very passionate and heated in their conversation. As they shared what they knew with those listening, everyone could tell something was different about these men. They were boldly proclaiming Jesus as Lord, and here's what happened: "When they observed the boldness of Peter and John and realized that they were uneducated and untrained men, they were amazed and recognized that they had been with Jesus" (Acts 4:13). Peter and John didn't have seminary degrees or formal education, but they were passionate about following Jesus, and it was obvious to everyone around them. Those people knew Peter and John had been with

Jesus. While formal education isn't a requirement for effective ministry, it's an incredible way to deepen your knowledge and skill base as you walk out the calling God has placed on your life.

I attended seminary to obtain a master's degree because I knew it was part of what God was calling me to do. Seminary was one of the richest seasons of my adult life. I'll forever be grateful for the tools I gained, the relationships that were built, the resources I had at my fingertips, and the overall confidence in what God was doing in my life. Could God be calling you to pursue more education or training opportunities?

Many of you have already taken advantage of college Bible classes, certificate courses, and seminary programs (many of which are online now) to further your education. I love that you've taken this next step! We've got to remain teachable in every season of our lives. Whether or not you ever set foot in another classroom, be a student who's always ready and willing to learn. Utilize conferences and other leadership opportunities that are at your fingertips, and always be a learner. You're already taking a step in that direction by reading this book. What's the next book on your list? What other ways are you growing "in wisdom and stature, and in favor with God and with people" like Jesus did (Luke 2:52)? Can the girls in your life tell that you're learning, growing, and spending time with Jesus?

At the heart of it, the call is to love on and disciple girls. This can be how you get started. It's easy to make things overcomplicated, but instead, just be obedient!

CHAPTER 6

IDENTIFY THE INROADS

Discipleship is not always glamorous or famous, but it is fruitful and eternal.

Discipleship can take place in a variety of different ways, so this chapter is designed to help point you to some of the practical things you can do to chart your path.

THROUGH THE CHURCH

As we point girls to Christ, let's also point them back to the local church. We see throughout the Book of Acts that the church is God's plan for accomplishing His purposes here on earth. The church isn't a building, but it's the body of believers. You don't need to have a job at your church to be a disciple maker, but are you connecting the dots back to the church? How can you be the hands and feet of Jesus to a group of teens? Show up where they are. Bring them with you. Teach them to love and serve the church.

At the beginning of each semester, I make it a point to ask girls for their sports and activity schedules, so I can try to make it to something they're participating in.

Are you a small group leader or Sunday school teacher? Y'all are my heroes. When I think back to when I was in middle and high school, they were honestly some of the most influential people in my life.

When we talk about discipleship through the church, it can look a variety of different ways. Some churches have discipleship programs through the student ministry or women's ministry that you can easily plug into and be paired with a girl or a group of girls to disciple. They often come with a set plan and structure, which some of you are looking for.

If your church doesn't currently have something like this, what if God is calling you to be the one to step up and lead? Talk to the person in leadership at your church to see if you can add to what they are already doing and help provide an avenue for discipleship in your church.

One key idea that I'll remind you of is to ask girls what they're looking for when they say they want to be discipled. Some of them may really be looking for Bible study, while others are looking for friendship and accountability. Knowing on the front end what they're looking for will help as you talk about expectations.

WHEN YOU'RE THE ONE IN CHARGE

Maybe you're the point person in your church—you're the girls minister on student ministry staff, a volunteer director, a student pastor's wife, or someone who just loves teen girls and has taken on the challenge!

Here are some practical ways you can take your discipleship program to the next level or simply kick it off!

- Lay out clear guidelines and expectations for both students and leaders.

- Provide a list of resource ideas for those who are looking for more of a Bible study driven group. (See list of resources at the back of this book.)

- Consider asking students to "apply" to be a part of a discipleship group— this gives you all of their info, but also helps you gauge where they are spiritually and what they need.

- Find ways to connect middle and high school girls with each other. If a high school girl is being discipled, see if she's ready to disciple a middle school girl. This gives her a great safety net and a resource to fall back on if she's already being discipled.

- Cast a vision for how you want to see discipleship grow—it's not just a club to join or something to be a part of for a short season, but it's so those being discipled will turn around and multiply their groups at the end of the time period.

- Find out what the rest of your church is doing (if you don't already know) as far as discipleship goes.

- Make sure everything you're doing falls under the umbrella of the mission and vision of your church.

I had the opportunity to spend almost two years investing in the life of a younger woman in ministry named Lauren Bush. Lauren has a clear calling on her life to ministry and at the time was serving as the girls ministry director at a local church. She reached out and asked if I would mentor her, and it was an absolute joy. I've watched her grow immensely in the Lord and in ministry over the last few years, and she has become a dear friend. Lauren never shied away from asking for honest feedback, and I love that about her. She has an incredibly teachable spirit. While she served as girls ministry director, she had the opportunity to establish a mentor program, and I think there's a lot we can learn from what she did.

LAUREN'S STORY:

I couldn't leave a coffee date or a Sonic run with a high school girl without feeling the weight of their desire to be noticed. They wanted someone to really see them, not because of their achievements, but because they are valuable in the eyes of the Lord. No matter how hard I tried, I knew I couldn't reach every girl. I recognized I needed to multiply myself in order to reach students and to see lives be impacted long after I was gone. This holy tension birthed the idea of starting a mentor program. I grabbed a couple of girls and leaders and went to the drawing board. After lots of prayer, think tank meetings, and a few pilot runs, we finally landed on something practical and fruitful.

The mentor program targeted high school girls in our church who wanted someone to walk alongside them and help them follow Jesus. I took some girls who were all-in with me to adult classes to have them share why mentoring matters and how women in our church can impact someone's life. Girls and adult mentors would sign-up online by filling out an application and a personality profile. My team placed people together based on the personality profiles, where they lived, and their schedules.

Once every girl was matched, I led a training session for the mentors to ensure they felt prepared and to create community with other mentors. Students and their parents got to meet their mentors at a luncheon called "The Mentor Reveal." It was a sweet opportunity for the girls, their parents, and their mentors to all share their story over a meal. The girls set spiritual goals, as the parents and mentors brainstormed how to help the students reach them. It set the stage for the mentor and the parents to collaborate together in discipling their high schooler.

The mentor would reach out to the girl each week to check in on her and see how she could be praying for her. This could be done through a phone call, a text message, or connecting face to face at church. Girls and their mentors would schedule a time to hang out each month for the remainder of the school year to discuss life and what they were learning from the Bible study resource I gave them. The mentors were prepped with a few open-ended questions to ask each time they were together just in case they weren't sure how to navigate through conversation. Most of the time, the mentors ended up simply listening because they created a space for girls to process and share. Several times a month, I would check in on my mentors to see how they were doing, to make myself available for coaching, and to see how I could learn from them. Over the course of the school year, the girls and their mentors had to participate in at least one Mentor Program Fellowship each semester on the church campus. Each month there was a scheduled mentor activity for the girls and their mentors to attend if they wanted to. It empowered the girls and the mentors to feel like they were all a part of something special in the church.

Did every mentor relationship work out perfectly? No. Some people just aren't going to mesh well, and that is OK! Was it messy at times? Yes. But every challenge along the way was worth it because girls got to tangibly see the pursuit of Jesus on their lives through their mentor. A win didn't consist of tons of girls signing up, but of seeing a heart treasure Jesus more today than it did yesterday. I cared more about girls having a safe space to wrestle with the truth of God's Word in some of their darkest moments than I did all the head knowledge they gained. Mentoring matters because it provides girls an opportunity to be truly seen by an older woman through the lens of the gospel.

Lauren also put together a handbook for the Mentor Program, and I love that she included these reminders to leaders:

- Pray for the girls and yourself!
- Partner with the family.
- Uplift the mom and dad and caretakers and make them the heroes.
- Take advantage of teachable moments.
- Set realistic goals and expectations.
- Reflect and rejoice on the sweet moments the Lord will provide.
- Remember you are not alone.
- Have fun!

Lauren's position at the church gave her an opportunity to lead in this, but what would a program like this look like in your local church?

> **What are a couple of things you can take away from Lauren's story? How might you apply these things to your local church?**

IN THE HOME

I'm not a mom, so I'm not even going to try to speak from experience as a mom here. I've asked a couple of moms to speak into this part so you can hear from them. As I've journeyed in girls ministry over the last decade, I've walked with and encouraged a lot of moms of teen girls. I know from my own experience as a teen that parenting one isn't easy, and it's not for the faint of heart. What I can tell you is that I'm so glad my parents loved me well, but didn't try to be my friends. They were my parents. Moms, be the mom; don't try to be a friend. There's only one of you, and your role is so critical!

I do feel like I can speak to having a mom who intentionally poured into and discipled me. It wasn't something formal or structured, but my mom set a great example of what following Jesus wholeheartedly looks like. I saw her spending time reading her Bible every morning, and she would often share with us something she learned or something she was praying specifically for. Mom still does this today—she'll often text me in the morning with a verse she read or how she's written in her prayer journal to pray for me that day. These things still mean the world to me. While I wasn't the easiest kid, my mom worked really hard to establish herself as the mom, but she became my friend over time. She wasn't easy on me, and I'm really thankful for it now. My parents both held me to a high standard, but they also gave me room to grow and learn. They set boundaries, but let me have some room to run around inside of those boundaries because they knew it was a safe place.

A lot of what I do now, I realize I learned by watching others along the way. So much of that watching came from seeing my mom pursue the Lord. I watched her take notes in church on Sunday, invite other families into our home as a gesture of kindness and hospitality, pray with those who were facing difficult seasons, and I also learned how to just show up when people need you. My mom would be the first to tell you she's not perfect, but she set a great example and modeled godliness for me in a way I hope I can pour into others and my future kids as well.

God placed parents over children and gave them the responsibility to disciple. No matter the home situation, kids and teens are disciples of something. Parents are the first line of defense, and their role is critical. In the Old Testament, we see the role of parents laid out clearly:

> *Love the Lord your God with all your heart, with all your soul, and with all your strength. These words that I am giving you today are to be in your heart. Repeat them to your children. Talk about them when you sit in your house and when you walk along the road, when you lie down and when you get up.* —Deuteronomy 6:5-7

The same truths are carried over to the New Testament when we see Paul reminding Timothy that his heritage of faith came from his grandmother Lois and his mother Eunice (2 Tim. 1:5). Because of the way they raised him, Timothy was now a fellow Christ follower.

We all know girls who come from homes where one or both parents don't have a relationship with Jesus. Our job isn't to try to be the parent or to take on that role, but to be a woman who can stand in the gap, pray, and encourage her to pursue Jesus. This also gives us an incredible opportunity to love on those parents as often we can, and pray that they would understand the truth of the gospel. While we don't bear the full weight of the responsibility, we can certainly pray fervently and be a godly influence in the lives of these girls.

Enough from me on this. Let's hear from a mom!

A MOM'S PERSPECTIVE

Diane Nix is a dear friend and discipler of countless women. If you were to hear her talk about her family, she would share that she has two biological daughters and two spiritual daughters. Those two spiritual daughters were birthed out of intentional discipleship relationships. I asked her to share with you why it's so crucial to disciple the daughters in your life.

DIANE'S STORY:

Today, discipling both my birth daughters and spiritual daughters is one of the highest privileges and challenges for me as a mom. It is a privilege to become the influence that speaks louder than any other voice in their head. The world is screaming for their attention. Your voice, cheering them on, challenging them, and most importantly praying them through, needs to be the loudest, clearest earthly voice they hear. This is a privilege you only have for a short time, and then like a snap of your fingers, it's gone. With this in mind, I'm okay having my voice in their head!

Discipling the girls has been a priority for me. It's through intentional mentoring (formal and informal at times), as well as investing in their spirits, souls, and bodies. Discipling is challenging because many women believe they have to be perfect in the role. The challenge is first surrendering all pretense to the Father and permitting Him to refine you as you disciple. The girls are watching you, whether they acknowledge it or not. True discipleship often happens at the most inopportune times. Times when you are living life, and it falls apart. Living daily life as you know the Lord would have you live. Letting them see your failures and your successes. When you fail, be honest and seek forgiveness (first from the Lord, and then if needed from her). Letting her watch you wrestle out your faith and having honest conversations are all a part of discipling your girls.

Discipling involves being their mom when they are screaming they want a best friend. Speaking the truth in love and challenging them to be the women God wants them to be. It also includes having their backs, whether you wholeheartedly agree or not. And finally, training young women to be who He has created them to be, despite what this world or even the church is saying. Discipleship is not always glamorous or famous, but it is fruitful and eternal.

AS YOU GO

When I've sought someone out to disciple me or someone has sought me out, it's been for a really clear-cut reason, and we're both way more apt to be all-in. For my personality, this approach has been most effective for me. You can always lean on your church staff for ideas and resources, but you're more on your own as far as coming up with a plan.

Maybe you're not a mom to a daughter, but would you be a spiritual mom to a girl? I have a few aunts and uncles in my life who aren't blood related, but they might as well be family. My Aunt Glenna fits this bill. She's the best storyteller I know, and we've made some incredible memories over the course of my life. My mom and Aunt Glenna have been best friends since I was five years old, so she's been present for just about everything in my life. She's more than just a friend—she's a second mom to me. Aunt Glenna stepped in for my mom on a couple of occasions when my mom couldn't be present, and I'm so thankful for her role in my life. When I was in second grade, we had a mother's day tea at school, but my brother was having surgery and my mom couldn't be there that day. So I invited Aunt Glenna to be my mom for the day. We made a chalkboard craft where I painted, "I love you, Mom" and it's sat in Aunt Glenna's kitchen window for as long as I can remember. When I got into middle school and high school, she would invite me to come work with her, and I loved every minute of it. While she was teaching me about her job, she was also teaching me about Jesus. She has been a wise counselor and friend my whole life, and I don't know what I would do without her. I've watched her walk through difficult situations with her head held high because she knows that God is faithful. Even though she doesn't have her own children, there are countless people who call her family and that she shows up for. She has been a faithful discipler of countless women by inviting them to do life with her. It's not complicated, but it's really intentional, and I'm incredibly grateful for her.

No matter how you're going about discipling girls, here are three key points to keep in mind:

1. IDENTIFY OPPORTUNITIES

What opportunities are right around you? Have you asked someone at your church where you can serve? Maybe you're the only one on staff at your church, and you're trying to figure out how you fit into the bigger picture of what God is doing in the lives of students. If you're a mom, what activities does your daughter participate in where you can meet other teen girls and women and make a connection? When is the last time you were on the soccer field sidelines actually having conversations with other people instead of staring at your phone or talking to your best friend?

2. RECOGNIZE MISSED OPPORTUNITIES

Missed opportunities are incredible learning tools. I want you to do some thinking back so you can then think forward. We're going to take a look at the last two weeks of your life. I'm going to ask you to be really objective as you answer these questions. We're all busy, we all love to occasionally binge watch a TV show, and sometimes our best way to decompress is to have some alone time. I'm just trying to help you think outside the box and see where some gaps may be to help you move forward.

Look at your calendar and list some of the places you've been over the last two weeks, outside of your home:

- Looking over your list, where are some places you could have brought a younger girl with you?

- Where are some time gaps in your schedule when you could have given to someone else?

- What are the things you do to fill time?

- Take a look at your phone—if it's anything like mine, there's a way to check how much time you've spent on each app. You can look at the last twenty-four hours and the last week. How much time did you spend on your phone?

- What shows or sports are you regularly watching? How many episodes or hours do you usually spend each week watching TV?

- Looking back at your answers, do you think you've missed any opportunities?

- How can you best honor God with the time you have?

3. EVALUATE YOUR COMMITMENT

I've learned over the last few years that it's really hard to say *no* to good things. Saying *no* to bad things is a much easier decision, but when I'm faced with good things, it's really hard to put a period at the end of the sentence and just say *no*. Two books that have really helped me as a recovering overcommitter are *Boundaries* by Henry Cloud and John Townsend and *The Best Yes* by Lysa TerKeurst. One of the things that stood out to me most in Lysa's book is the idea that sometimes our *no* opens up the door for someone else to say *yes*. If you're overcommitted but want to disciple, what needs to be cleared off your plate so you have the time and energy to pour into someone else?

If there aren't any visible gaps in your schedule, consider the following:

- Are you currently overcommitted?

- What are some things you can do to make a change?

- Is there anything you can take a step back from for a season?

- Is God being honored in everything you're giving your time to, or are you just spinning your wheels?

- How can you best honor God with your time?

However you go about it, don't miss the opportunity to make disciples of the girls in your life. Different seasons will give way to more or less time than we can commit, but we are no less called to make disciples because of the season of our lives. Friend, do what you can with what you have. No one is looking for perfection, but we're all looking for other women in our lives who will help us be more like Christ.

Who are the girls you're already around?

Where do you see the Lord leading you to begin discipling?

CHAPTER 7

NAVI-GATING REAL LIFE

Whatever you're facing, be faithful right where He has placed you. God is fully aware of your circumstances, and nothing catches Him off guard.

Now that we've addressed some first steps and creating connections, let's talk about some details.

If you're going to be more structured, set a regular time to get together and meet with the girl or girls you are discipling. I've found that one of the most helpful things you can do for girls is set the expectations on the front end. Let them know what you expect from them, but also what they can also expect from you. Believe it or not, most teens function best within boundaries. They're waiting on someone to draw a line that will catch them if they try to run too far—will you be the one to do it? There's a good chance that some of them will push the boundaries and expectations to see if you're actually going to follow through. If you do follow through, it shows them you mean business. If you don't follow through and just let things slide, there's a good chance they'll quit on you. Teens are looking for adults who are good on their word and remain trustworthy. Don't be surprised if you are put to the test right off the bat. So many girls have faced disappointment, and they want to know if you're going to do the same.

What kind of expectations are you going to set for yourself and for the girl or girls you're discipling?

Here are some examples:

- Set a regular time to meet. As the leader, put it on your calendar and don't miss it unless you absolutely have to.

- Commit to meet even if some of your girls aren't going to be there. This helps them to understand that you're all in.

- Let them know what you're going to do when you meet and what they need to accomplish for the next time (e.g., ask accountability questions, memorize Scripture, ask about quiet times, and so on.).

Reflect back on a time as a teen when someone you trusted failed to meet your expectations. How did that make you feel?

What safeguards can you put into place for yourself as a leader so you don't do the same thing to the girl or girls you are discipling?

PERSONAL DISCIPLESHIP

One of the most important things you can do is continue to be discipled yourself. We serve best out of the overflow of what God is doing in our lives. I don't know about you, but serving and ministering from a dry place is difficult. It's not impossible, but it's not easy, and it's really exhausting over time.

When was the last time you remember feeling spiritually filled up?

List some things you do to make sure you stay filled up.

I've experienced such dry seasons that I honestly didn't even remember what it was like to feel filled up. I recently went to our local farmer's market and finally got up the courage to speak to the man selling herbs. Over the last few months, I've thought so many times about planting a few herbs on our patio, but I'm so afraid I'm going to kill them. With a good bit of trepidation, I walked up to the man and said, "If I have a black thumb, which of these herbs am I least likely to kill?" He chuckled and asked me what kind of herbs I like. After listing off a few, he immediately told me not to try to grow cilantro (which is honestly the one I wanted so badly because hello, salsa!), but plants like mint and basil are much harder to kill. He warned me that most people overwater their herbs. He made me promise that if I bought the plants, I wouldn't overwater them, and I told him I would try my best. The man also said something that I have thought about so much over the last few weeks: "You can underwater the plant and still bring it back to life, but if you overwater it, you're probably going to kill it. If it starts to look and feel dry, give it some water and it will quickly perk back up." So often, I'm the dry plant that needs the Living Water to pick me back up. While there's no such thing as overwatering in the Christian life, we can definitely do things that will cause us to drown, and it's really hard to recover.

As Christ followers, we have to be fed and watered with the Word of God on a regular basis to thrive. Consistent, daily watering is what is keeping these herbs alive, and it's the same for us. The world can do its best to totally drown us, but regular time with God creates an environment in which we can grow and multiply. Many of you probably feel like you've already been drowned, and therefore, you're disqualified. That couldn't be further from the truth.

HOW DO I CHOOSE A BIBLE STUDY?

I get asked this question a lot, and I always respond with, "Tell me about the girls in your group. What do they need?" There are so many great options out there—some of them have homework, some have videos, some walk through books of the Bible, some are topical, but you have to know the girls you're leading. Look at the next few weeks and months, know what kind of commitment you've asked for, and ask the girls what they're looking for. Oftentimes, asking them the question or giving them options is a great place to start. In the back of the book, you'll find a list of resources.

HOW SHOULD I DEAL WITH DIFFICULT SITUATIONS?

I'm going to give you some fair warning—this isn't always going to be easy. It would be naive of me to not address some of the difficult things that come with discipleship. Spiritual warfare, drama, inconsistency, lying, sin issues, addiction, and trauma are just the beginning of the list. While you can't be prepared for whatever situation comes, your job is to be attentive to the Lord and to the girls He has entrusted to you. I'll never forget the day one of our high school girls, who I hadn't seen in a couple of months came and found me on a Sunday morning. I was so glad to see her, and she immediately looked at me and said, "I need to tell you I'm pregnant." In most situations, my normal reaction right then would be, "Congratulations!" But I had to be a wise friend and girls minister in this moment and respond by giving her a hug and sitting down to talk. A girl I was discipling that same year came to me in tears to tell me she'd been sleeping with her boyfriend. It was a teachable moment she opened the door to, but I didn't feel totally prepared. We sat down to talk, and it led to more conversations over the next few weeks. I was so thankful both of these girls chose to trust me with something difficult they were walking through, and they let me be a part of their story as it continued to unfold.

When a girl shares something difficult with you, be a good listener. That's usually never the right moment to reprimand and correct, but to hear her out. Thank her for sharing something difficult with you, and set a time to get together within the next couple of days so you can continue the conversation. This gives you time to seek the Lord and seek wise counsel from others if you need to. Be wise about when and how you ever share something confidential with someone else, so you don't lose the trust of a girl who has just taken a huge step to share with you.

One summer, we were really having modesty issues with the girls in our student ministry. It was right when Nike shorts came out, and let's just be honest – they were a little too short, especially after you roll them three times. Our student ministry team decided to interview some high school guys about modesty and how it affected them, and I happened to be sitting in the editing room when our video guy was putting the whole video together. After flipping through the footage and explaining what we were looking for, he turned to me and said, "The more these girls fall in love with Jesus, the less things like this are going to be an issue." It's a conversation that stopped me in my tracks. I'll never forget it.

So often, we're trying to remedy the symptoms, but not the root issue. At its core, it's not a modesty issue.

It's a heart issue.

A Holy Spirit issue.

A relationship with Jesus issue.

Does a relationship with Jesus mean we're never going to sin? No. Does it mean that we've got it all figured out? Absolutely not. It means that we're ever becoming more like Him, and we're changed as a result.

WHAT DO I DO WHEN IT GETS HARD?

When it gets hard, beg the Lord to give you wisdom. Ask Him how to move forward. Be one who gives grace, but also speaks truth. When it gets hard, don't immediately walk away. Be faithful where you are. My friend Lauren says there's a good chance that's what my family will write on my tombstone, because I say it all the time. Our calling is to be faithful right where God has planted us until He releases us for something else. Whatever you're facing, be faithful right where He has placed you. God is fully aware of your circumstances, and nothing catches Him off guard. Ask Him for wisdom, and trust Him with the direction He gives you.

HOW DO I KNOW WHEN TO INVOLVE A COUNSELOR?

Molly Moore is one of my best friends from seminary, and now she's a licensed professional counselor (and she's pretty awesome), so I asked her to help us better understand when it's the right time to involve a counselor when you're dealing with difficult situations. If you're a parent, keep your ears open and don't miss when people are pointing out something you might not see. If you're not a parent, be wise and don't be afraid to raise a red flag to parents if you see something they need to be aware of.

MOLLY'S STORY:

Many wonder when the right time to seek a counselor is. My experience has often been that, if you are questioning whether you should see a counselor, you probably should. A common misconception is that you only need to see a counselor if things are absolutely terrible or if you are crazy. Neither could be further from the truth. The term "counselor" is a translation of the word parakletos *that is often used by the apostle John in the New Testament. Rather than being a specific title, it expresses a function—to assist, support, counsel or advise. This is how I see my role as a counselor—one who comes alongside whoever is in my office and offer whatever is needed for that individual. Some just need someone to listen and be present. Others are lacking the coping skills needed to face whatever adversities they are facing and need new and/or healthier ideas to try. Another misconception many have is that by going to counseling, they will be sucked in and have to go for the rest of their lives. This is a false assumption. The longer I am a counselor, the more I am convinced that we all need counseling at different points in our lives, counselors included. We all face times that are hard and push us beyond what we know how to process. But that does not mean we all need to be in counseling on a weekly basis forever. I very much believe that it can be appropriate for certain seasons in our lives, but seasons come and go. Many only need to come to counseling for a season, and then they feel prepared to stop. It is always a case-by-case situation, depending on the things they have faced in their lives and the coping skills they have in place to deal with those things.*

If you do choose to seek counseling, be sure to assure teen girls that you don't think they are crazy, that it will not be forever, and that a counselor is just a good resource for them to learn and grow and become the best version of themselves. It also gives them a confidential adult that will be unbiased and there for them.

When working with teens and families, my first suggestion is to always see a doctor first. Sometimes behaviors and problems can have a somatic origin, meaning they could be a result of a deficiency or other medical problem that could be easily solved, so I always recommend my clients see a medical professional first to rule out any medical conditions. If these issues have been ruled out, a counselor can help a myriad of concerns that may be facing teens. Some of the most common issues I see in my office are depression, bullying (recipient of or cause of), grief, trauma, family problems, and anxiety. Due to the presence of unlimited forms of social media and supposed constant connection, teens are facing a pressure that previous generations have never known. The constant pressure of comparing themselves to their friends online exhausts many. Kids and adults, alike, only post the best versions of their days online, so it seems as though everyone has it together. Knowing you do not seems like failure.

When looking for a counselor, be careful to make sure the people who will be speaking into your teen's life are people that will speak truth, first and foremost. Look for counselors who will connect with your teen and have some understanding of the culture they are in or a willingness to learn. Besides the benefits of being able to work through the issues the girl may be facing, a counselor can also be a good interpreter and/or mediator between parents and child. In situations where there may be family disagreements or behavior problems, my experience is almost always that both parent and child are not happy with how things are going, but neither knows how to get out of the cycle they seem to be in. A counselor is a good person to help strategize new tactics and interpret each other's experiences to the parent and child. Another benefit to counseling teens is that you are building positive role models into their lives, so as they grow and face a myriad of issues that come with growing up, they have a trusted unbiased third party person that has proven they will listen, not judge and encourage them, but still point them towards truth. As long as you find a counselor that is trustworthy and can build a good rapport with your teen, the positives to seeking a counselor could be limitless, with few negatives, if any. I may be biased, but I think a counselor is always a good idea if you are considering whether or not your teen needs it.

RECOGNIZING THE ROLE
OF PARENTS

I'm so thankful for the role my parents played in my spiritual life and development, but I'm also thankful they set me free to be invested in by other women. Maybe you're a mom reading this today and trying to figure out the balance of discipling your daughter and letting other women disciple her as well. If you're a mom—set your daughter free to be poured into by other women. I hope you'll find encouragement from my friend Kim Smith as she shares her story of why she believes it's important to let other women pour into her daughter, Hannah.

KIM'S STORY:

I believe it is vital to my daughter's spiritual growth and long term well-being to have other godly role models pour into her life. She has been blessed to have this in every stage of her life, whether it be an aunt, her grandmother, an older student, a teacher, her girls minister, or one of my friends. Simply by encouraging her or spending time with her, they help shape and define who God has created her to be. They speak truth into her life, so she will recognize a lie from the enemy as he tries to speak into her life. They help her become more alert to unbiblical thinking, habits that might harm her, and unwise behavior. They speak into her the value of who God has created her to be, and therefore, encourage self-worth in her. These women help her understand her strengths and weaknesses and intentionally move her toward God. Their encouragement gives her a place of acceptance and security, a place where she feels safe to be herself. In a world with so many distractions and so many examples of broken icons, she needs to see those who have made godly decisions and entrusted their lives to Jesus above all else. When they share their life experiences with her, they are teaching her to navigate life with the strength, wisdom, and grace of God. They are living examples of those who have made intentional choices to go against the grain of society, but also love those who aren't in that same place. They show her there is great strength in weakness and that God will carry her through difficult times. I would be foolish to think my words and prayers alone are enough to shape her heart and mind. As a mom, it gives me great peace to know God is still writing her story, and He is using other godly women to guide her along her journey.

I'm so thankful for women like Kim who have invested in me over the years. When I was young in ministry, Kim and her husband, Michael (I'll tell you about him in chapter 10), came to serve on our student ministry team, and they so quickly let me be a part of their family. Kim is one of the women who I've learned a ton from over the years, and it was during a season when I lived at home and worked after college. I'm so thankful that even then, my mom encouraged me to spend time with women like her, and I'm better of because of it. Kim and I have walked through a lot of life together over the last ten years, including the death of her husband, Michael. A lot of our friendship was forged out of difficult situations, but I wouldn't be who I am today without the Smith family. Hannah is like a little sister to me and stood by my side as a junior bridesmaid when I got married. I loved learning from watching them up close over the years. If your daughter wants to spend time around godly people, pray about letting her do just that.

If you're not a mom, part of our job is to respect the roles of parents. Our job is to be a cheerleader and a helper, but not to parent students. You have an incredible opportunity to lead well, but not to lead them away from their parents.

CHAPTER 8

HELP HER FLOURISH

As you dig deeper into the Word, you will undoubtedly fall more in love with Jesus.

One way to start digging in with the girls you are discipling is by helping them understand what spiritual disciplines look like in our lives. There are some awesome resources out there that have been a huge help to me in this area over the years. Two of my favorite books are Spiritual Disciplines for the Christian Life *by Donald Whitney and* Celebration of Discipline *by Richard Foster. While there's not a master list of what makes a spiritual discipline, there are key things we see throughout Scripture that show us the way we should walk. As you walk through these things with girls and young women, don't be surprised if you see growth in your own life as a result.*

READING THE BIBLE

The Bible can be pretty intimidating. It's filled with big words, parables, and measurements that can be hard to understand. And sometimes all those things keep us from really digging into Scripture. Many of us have participated in Bible studies but have never taken the step of learning how to read and study the Bible, much less taught someone else how to read and study.

A few years ago, I read through the Bible chronologically, and it was one of the richest seasons in Bible study I've ever had. As I read, I saw everything unfold as one huge story, which all points to Jesus. It's simply beautiful.

Here are nine things to consider as you study the Bible and lead girls to do the same:

1. ***Know what you're getting into.*** People will often study Scripture asking the question, "What does this passage mean to me?" when the better question would be, "What does this passage mean?" The interpretation of the Bible isn't up to us and our best guess as to what it might or could mean; God inspired it with a specific interpretation, and our goal should be discerning what that is.

2. Pray before you study. This may seem obvious or redundant, but it's critical. When we approach Scripture, it should be with humility and an attitude to receive and learn. Ask God to reveal Himself to you through His Word. We are given the Holy Spirit as a guide as we interpret the Word (Acts 2).

3. Choose a plan. For those of you who like some structure, there are a ton of resources available. Here are some great places to start: The One Year Bible, She Reads Truth, or YouVersion. These plans will walk you through the Bible and can be a great way to start or enhance your journey of studying Scripture.

4. Read the passage in context. It can be easy to just pick out a verse that sounds good to you, but to really understand it, you should read the context (the surrounding chapter/verses). Take the time to find out who the author is, who the book was written to, and why it was written. This can clear up a lot of questions. A study Bible or commentary can be a great resource.

5. Interpret Scripture by Scripture. Hang with me on this one. In *Essential Truths of the Christian Faith*, R.C. Sproul writes, "We must not set one passage of Scripture against another passage. Each text must be understood not only in light of its immediate context but also in light of the context of the whole of Scripture."[1] When you can look at Scripture as one big story, all inspired by God, you will start to see it more clearly.

6. Approach the Bible with a teachable spirit. If I've learned anything over the last few years, it's how much I don't know. There are a lot of things about the Bible we have to wrestle over. We're grappling with concepts and truths about theology and doctrine, and it's hard. Sometimes, we're just trying to understand a basic truth. It's important to dig and ask questions, but knowing we can't (with our finite minds) completely understand it all. Continue to ask hard questions, and don't give up!

7. Allow God to speak. So often, we approach the Bible with a "what's in it for me?" attitude. Don't just read to check it off a list, but read to understand and learn. The Word begins to come alive as you start to soak it in. As you spend time in the Word daily, it allows God to speak to you through His Word.

8. Take it slow and ask questions. You're not going to understand it all in one day! If you prefer a verse-by-verse approach, study God's Word that way. Don't be afraid to ask questions—it's a huge part of the learning process. The more you read and study, the more the Bible will come alive in your life.

9. Be a student of the Word. Be in the Bible daily. Make sure you have people in your life who are at least a little bit ahead of you in their spiritual journey. Ask someone to disciple you and to challenge you as you study the Bible.

As you dig deeper into the Word, you will undoubtedly fall more in love with Jesus. My prayer for you is that you develop a love for God's Word that is unquenchable, and that it spreads to the girls you're discipling. The impact of seeing how the Bible has changed your life will give great opportunities for girls to ask questions and gain some valuable tools as they're growing and learning.

PRAYER

Prayer is vital in the life of Christ followers. It's the way we communicate with God, and it's how we intercede on behalf of others. Scripture tells us we have a "great High Priest" (Heb. 4:14) who goes before God on our behalf. As believers, we are also intercessors for the people in our lives. We are given not only the opportunity and responsibility, but also the privilege of praying for people and situations. Prayer is a crucial spiritual discipline in our lives but can be challenging to put into practice. Putting prayer into practice in a way that girls can see will provide moments when they can move beyond praying for their cats and best friends to praying more intentionally. They will begin to model what they see in front of them, and you've been given a space to help make it happen.

I have a lot of friends who journal their prayers. It's something I've tried off and on, but it's hard for me. So often, people ask us to pray for something, but we never write it down or remember to actually pray for the need. By writing it down you can keep track of what you're praying for and see how God answers prayers. One of my favorite things to do is go back and see God's faithfulness and His hand at work over time. When you keep a record of requests you're praying for, it's easy to see what He's up to.

Here are just a few ideas to help you develop the practice of prayer in your life and lead girls to do the same:

- If you feel comfortable and are able, get on your knees or lay prostrate on the floor when you pray. Your physical posture is one way you can express the posture of your heart.

- Praise God for who He is—don't just start asking God to do things for you. Acknowledge who He is and all He has done.

- Pray specifically. God cares about details and wants to know what's on your heart.

- Confess your sins. Just be honest and lay it all out there. It can be really hard to do, but hear the truth of 1 John 1:9 when it says, "If we confess our sins, he is faithful and just to forgive us our sins and to cleanse us from all unrighteousness."

- Integrate Scripture into your prayer as a way of speaking God's promises back to Him and declaring truth.

- Follow the model of the Lord's Prayer (Matt. 6).

- Pray out loud. I often do this on my way to work in the mornings. It's easy to get distracted when we only pray silently, but there's power in the name of Jesus and in speaking our prayers out loud.

- Surrender your prayers to God and leave them at His feet. While it's easy to pray that God would answer prayers in a specific way, we have to trust Him with the outcome. This is much easier said than done, but in the words of my oh-so-wise mom, "I trust the Lord way more than I trust myself."

- As you pray for answers, pray that your will would be aligned with His. The more we seek God and follow Him wholeheartedly, the more our will starts looking less and less like a list of our wants and desires, but looks more like God's desires for us.

- "Wait for the LORD; be strong, and let your heart be courageous; wait for the LORD" (Ps. 27:14).

Often, waiting can be the most challenging part of prayer. We wait because we trust. As we wait, we give glory to the One who created us, formed us, and still communicates with us through His Word and through prayer. As you teach girls to pray, they'll likely look to you in the waiting. How you wait will model what waiting looks like for them. Don't miss this opportunity to share with them the real-life part of prayer, even when it's hard.

MEMORIZING SCRIPTURE

"Memorizing Scripture is so easy," said no one ever (or at least not anyone I know). It takes a lot of discipline to memorize Scripture on a consistent basis.

While it's not always the easiest thing, it's such a crucial spiritual discipline that helps me grow in my walk with the Lord. This is also a vital tool you can use as you disciple girls. Helping them understand the importance of memorizing Scripture while actually putting it into practice.

In *Spiritual Disciplines for the Christian Life* by Donald Whitney, he shares that "When Scripture is stored in the mind, it is available for the Holy Spirit to bring to your attention when you need it most ... What Christian doesn't want his or her faith strengthened? One thing you can do to strengthen it is to discipline yourself to memorize Scripture."[2]

Here are a few key things that have been helpful when it comes to memorizing Scripture:

- *Accountability*—Have someone ask you how you're doing and set deadlines for yourself. Discipleship is a great avenue for this. You can hold each other accountable and use the verses you memorize as encouragement along the way.

- *Repetition, repetition, repetition*—For some of you, this means writing the verse out several times, and for others, it's saying it out loud. It may even be helpful for you to draw a picture that reminds you of the verse. Find your learning style and use what works best for each person.

- *Meditate*—Spend time reflecting on the meaning of the verse. Don't just memorize it without looking at the context to see what's really happening. Make sure you know the bigger picture, and it will usually give you a better understanding of the verse you're memorizing. This is a great teaching tool for you to use so you fully understand what you're learning.

- **Make it visible**—For me, I often put my verse on an index card above my steering wheel or on the mirror in my bathroom. Sometimes, I take a picture of the verse with my phone and use it as the background. Find what works for you!

- **Choose a meaningful verse**—Find a verse that applies to your life. Is there a verse you've read recently in your Bible study that really stands out to you? Use that one!

- **Do the verse justice**—Make it a point to know all of the words and even the punctuation. It's all there for a reason! It will also help you in the long run to know you really know the verse, as well as the reference.

FASTING

I had a hard time taking on this section because seasons of fasting in my life are some of my favorite "good secrets" that I have with God. I really feel like He prompted me to share three things with you: What Scripture says about fasting, what He has taught me through the discipline of fasting, and an encouragement to make it a regular part of your spiritual life as you lead girls.

WHAT SCRIPTURE SAYS ABOUT FASTING

In the Sermon on the Mount found in the Gospel of Matthew, Jesus teaches about fasting. He says, "Whenever you fast, don't be gloomy like the hypocrites. For they make their faces unattractive so that their fasting is obvious to people. Truly I tell you, they have their reward. But when you fast, put oil on your head and wash your face, so that your fasting isn't obvious to others but to your Father who is in secret. And your Father who sees in secret will reward you" (Matt. 6:16-18).

There's a difference between good secrets and bad secrets, and fasting is a good secret. If you've never fasted before, it's one of the most intimate times with God I've ever experienced. When we forgo food, there's a dependency on Jesus that we can't explain. He literally becomes the Bread of life in a new way.

The passage above is just one example of countless references throughout the Old and New Testaments about fasting. I looked up the word for "fast" in Strong's Concordance, and when you translate the Greek word nēsteuō it means "to abstain from food."[3] Pretty straightforward if you ask me! Throughout Scripture, we see many occasions where people are fasting and praying for those who are sick or who have a great need. Other times, it's for an answer to prayer or for intimate time with God. When we forgo food and spend intentional time with God, He has our attention, and we're more apt to listen. We watched Jesus model this for us in the Gospels, especially when He fasted for forty days in the desert (Matt. 4:1-11).

Here are some examples of fasting in Scripture: Ezra 8:21; Ezra 9:5; Nehemiah 1:4; Esther 4:3; Psalm 69:10; Isaiah 58; Daniel 9:3; Joel 2:12; Matthew 4:2; Acts 13:2-3; Acts 14:23.

MY EXPERIENCE

I had a hard time figuring out how to write this part because we've just talked about fasting being a secret. But I feel the Lord prompted me to share this with you, and I hope you'll see it as a teaching point and an encouragement. There have been several occasions where the Lord has called me into long seasons of fasting. These weren't by my choice but by a very clear prompting of the Holy Spirit, which He confirmed. I cried when I felt like God was calling me to fast for longer periods of time because honestly, I love food. It represents fellowship with friends and family to me, and I knew the season was going to look radically different from normal. After talking to several godly men and women who prayed over me and with me, God confirmed through the reading of Scripture and the teaching of His Word that this was exactly what He was calling me to do.

I won't go into great detail, but I look back on that time period and remember how challenging it was. Yet it was also one of the richest seasons of my spiritual walk with God. He spoke to me so clearly as I dove into the Bible and used that season as preparation for a very difficult season that was quickly to follow. He used that time to reshape my heart and truly make it new. I had to be completely dependent on the Lord. There were days I wanted to quit, and I really had to grab onto the fact that God had called me to do this and He would sustain me.

In other seasons, I've fasted for one day a week or one day a month. Don't feel like fasting has to be for a long period of time, but be open to fasting when the Lord leads.

WHAT DOES THIS LOOK LIKE FOR YOU?

Don't ask God "if" He wants you to fast, but how and when to fast. Scripture is clear that it's a part of our relationship with Him. Matthew 6:16 says "when you fast," not "if." Some of you have medical conditions that prevent you from fasting from food—and that's fine! What is something else in your life you can lay on the altar in order to spend more time with God? For those of you who can fast from food, don't choose something else to fast from just because it seems easier than giving up food. When we see fasting in Scripture, it's always from food.

Fasting is a part of our love and worship to our Savior. He is worth it, and He is more than worthy of it! Maybe He's calling you to fast one meal a week or one day a week. Maybe it's once a month. Some of my single friends have spent one day a week fasting for their future husbands. Maybe you have a sick family member or friend you can fast and pray for.

Whenever you do fast, don't boast about it. It can be one of the sweetest secrets between you and the Lord. Certainly don't lie about it, but ask God for a way to say something like, "Thanks for inviting me to lunch, but I'm just going to stay in today." When you do fast, don't pick up your phone to scroll or just keep working through lunch. Get into the Word! Spend time praying and asking God to move and to speak clearly to you. If you put yourself in a position to hear from Him, I believe you will. For some of you, God will give you clarity on discipleship through fasting. Whatever your need and reason, give it over to Him, and see how He uses it for His glory.

As you live out this discipline, you'll be able to teach girls what it looks like and encourage them on their own journeys. I learned about fasting because I saw women around me fasting, and I wanted to know more. They weren't bragging about it, but it provided an opportunity for me to ask questions and better understand this particular spiritual discipline. If you've never tried this before, do it and see what God does.

WORSHIP

A couple of years ago I heard a worship song that I have since played over and over and over and over again. It's "Good, Good Father" by Housefires (featuring Pat Barrett), and I think I've finally realized why I love the song so much. It's because it declares who God is. It declares His goodness to His people, and because of His goodness, we see who we are in light of who He is.

When we declare who God is, we find ourselves at the heart of worship. It's reflecting back to God who He is. It's fixing our eyes on Him in a way that infiltrates every other area of our lives. When we live in a constant state of worship, it's more than a song. It changes the way we do everything. The way we talk to our friends and family, the way we approach a hard conversation, and how we respond to situations with the girls in our lives. At the end of the day, it's about bringing glory to God in everything we say and do.

It's easy to engage in worship at church or during a conference, but are we really worshiping God with our lives? We are called to worship the One who has released us from our shackles, given us freedom, and allows us to be a part of the story of redemption He's writing. It's not optional for believers, but a part of our relationship with God.

He is worthy of our praise and adoration, but there are seasons in our lives when it's hard to worship (Ps. 96:4). Maybe you've lost a job, faced a miscarriage, separated from your husband, or have been hurt by a friend. When we face difficulty, we have a choice to make. Am I going to focus on myself in this moment, or am I going to focus on God and who He is? Sister, He is glorified in our pain and suffering. Psalm 147:3 says, "He heals the brokenhearted and binds up their wounds." He is with us when we cry ourselves to sleep at night. He is the comforter in our sadness and loneliness.

The girls in our lives have most likely been exposed to worship, but do they understand why we worship, and why it matters? Do they see worship as "what we do at youth group" or "that part of church when everyone closes their eyes and raises their hands"? Is worship genuine to them, or do they see worship as something completely disconnected from the rest of their lives?

We are all going to face challenging seasons in our lives. It's really easy to make the choice to focus on how difficult it is, how I feel hurt, and how much I wish things were different. Let me tell you, it doesn't help. I just end up feeling miserable. When I feel those emotions coming on, I try to start declaring who God is. I declare that He is good (Ps. 136:1), He is faithful (1 Cor. 1:9), and He is for me (Rom. 8:31). He hasn't forgotten me (Isa. 49:15-16). I put Scripture in front of my face, so I can't forget the truth. When we do this, girls are going to notice. They're going to see our strength in trials and want to know more.

Worship is not a fight between contemporary or traditional music, instruments or a cappella, lyrics on a screen or hymnals, dresses or jeans, but it's about God—who He is and what He has done for us. Worship isn't about us at all.

You have an incredible opportunity to show the girls in your life what it looks like to live a life abandoned to worshiping God. This doesn't mean you have to go to a contemporary church and raise your hands during every song—it means your life tells the story of who God is and what He has done for us. Worship goes so far beyond church on Sunday mornings or a Hillsong United concert. We all worship something or someone—can the girls in your life tell who or what you worship?

No matter how long you've been a follower of Christ, we all still have a lot to learn. You may have been practicing these things for years or decades, or you may be brand new to some of this. Wherever your starting point, we have a responsibility to show the next generation the way by pointing them to Jesus. One of my friends recently shared with me that my relationship with God is one of the things that caused her to fall more in love with Jesus over the last few years. This floored me, and reminded me that living out our faith no matter where we are is unbelievably important. Girls are watching, and they often need us to go back to the basics as we help them navigate growing in faith. Whether by structure or intention, or just sharing our lives, spiritual disciplines will lead to growth in us and the girls we lead.

CHAPTER 9

EQUIP HER

Discipleship is teaching and modeling and passing on to others what was passed down to us.

Remember in chapter five when we talked about the passage in Acts 8 about Philip and the Ethiopian eunuch? Let's revisit this story. Because Philip was obedient to the Holy Spirit, he was able to share the good news of Jesus with a man who didn't yet know it. There are girls in your life right now who need to know who Jesus truly is. Many of them only know what they have been told by someone, whether it's good or bad.

My mom (whether she realizes it or not) is one of the most effective disciplers of younger women I know, but she's the real deal. If I had a dollar for every time one of my friends asked me if she could call my mom for wisdom or advice, I'd be able to buy each of you a Sonic drink. Her name is Shugie (yes, it's a nickname), but I call her The Shug. Her faithfulness to follow Jesus with all of her heart has set an example for me in more ways than I can count. One of the sweetest things at this stage of my life is watching my mom have opportunities to reach out and minister to women in her church and community. She co-leads a ministry to young moms at her church, and it has been an incredible opportunity to share Jesus with women who don't know Him. A few months ago, she called to ask me to pray because she was taking a girl to lunch at Chick-fil-A that didn't know Jesus. She said, "I'm really praying that sometime soon God will give me an opportunity to share the gospel with her. I'm just not sure when." I paused for a second and said, "Mom, today is the day. The opportunity is right in front of you."

We keep praying for opportunities, but we somehow can't see the opportunities that are right in front of our faces. Have you prayed for opportunities to share the gospel with girls you know? Or have you prayed that God would give you eyes to see the girls you can reach out to and connect with? If you haven't, today is a great day to start. If you have been praying something along these lines, be expectant that God will move!

I asked one of my student ministry heroes to share a story in this chapter because I want you to hear from a pastor's perspective. Keith Harmon is the first student pastor I served under, and he and his wife Jackie have been some of my greatest cheerleaders in ministry. I learned so much from watching them do ministry and I'm eternally grateful for the ways they have discipled me over the years.

KEITH'S STORY:

I was a student pastor for twenty-one years with groups ranging from twenty students in weekly attendance to over 1,000 students in weekly attendance. Four years ago, I had the privilege of transitioning to Marriage and Family Pastor at Cross Church Springdale, and my wife Jackie serves alongside me in this new area of ministry. It never mattered to me whether our ministry had twenty students or 1,000 students; the two non-negotiables for me were evangelism and discipleship. We built every ministry we have ever been a part of on those two non-negotiables, and we are doing the same thing with Marriage and Family Ministry. Evangelism and Discipleship go hand in hand, and they are really married to one another.

Discipleship is important because Jesus told us to be about it. Matthew 28:18-20 says, "Jesus came near and said to them, 'All authority has been given to me in heaven and on earth. Go, therefore, and make disciples of all nations, baptizing them in the name of the Father and of the Son and of the Holy Spirit, teaching them to observe everything I have commanded you. And remember, I am with you always, to the end of the age.'"

When I showed up in Anderson, Missouri as a twenty-three-year-old, full-time student pastor for the very first time in my life, I told the four adult workers and thirteen teens that we were going to reach that city and their schools by doing two things: winning people to Jesus and then discipling them. We did just that, and God blessed it. We did the same thing at every church God took us to after that, and God always does His part! We saw students saved, and then we taught them the Bible. We taught them to love and care about the things God loves and cares about.

Very early in my student ministry career I learned I could not disciple every student God brought to us by myself. I learned the importance of partnering with other adults, college students, and parents with a heart to win students to Jesus and then disciple them. Evangelism has always come easy, but I had to work hard at personal discipleship. Winning people to the Lord and helping them with the first steps of obedience comes fairly natural for me, but discipling others, as much as I enjoy it, is more difficult. That is another reason partnering with others is so important. We need each other. This is how God uses the body of Christ! Since I became a Christian, I have always had a small group of guys I have poured into spiritually. This was done for me, and then I was encouraged to do it for others. It was modeled for me, so I did not know any different.

If we really want someone to grow in his or her walk with Christ and if we really want the church to grow, we must learn to disciple others, and we must learn to partner with others to do it. I was fortunate to have a college student and other adults pour into me after I was saved as a 16-year-old high school boy. Much of what I do in ministry today, I learned from the men and women God placed in my life who poured into me as a young Christian, and now I am able to pass that along to others.

Discipleship is important because the church (the body of Christ) cannot and will not grow without it. If we want this generation of believers to have a heart for the Great Commission, a heart for God, and a heart for the Great Commandment, we must teach them and model what that looks like. If we want them to live a missional lifestyle, we must model that for them. If we want them to be great "churchmen" (and women) who attend, invite, serve, give and even go, we must teach them. This is called discipleship! Discipleship is not just going through a book or a particular study, although those are great tools. Discipleship is teaching and modeling and passing on to others what was passed down to us.

REACHING OUT

You don't have to be in full-time ministry to help the girls in your life be effective when it comes to evangelism, you just have to be willing. Chances are, they know girls who don't know Jesus. They're at every school lunch, football game, mall, and movie theater. They're friends with girls who do know and love Jesus, so they're right in their path. We just have to help girls learn to be intentional enough to invite and include them. It would be really easy for us to gear everything we do around the church girl, but we're really missing an incredible opportunity to reach the lost girl, too. I really believe you can do both things at the same time.

One way to effectively reach the lost girl is to share the gospel with her. Don't hesitate to share the truth of who Jesus is and why He came to die on the cross for our sins, and how He was resurrected from the dead three days later. This story has power, so let the story do the work! You just need to be willing to share. When you are obedient to share, it allows the girls to see the powerful simplicity of the gospel. They often learn by seeing, which then gives them confidence to do the same. We all are called to be evangelists and ministers of the gospel. It may seem to come to some people more easily, but it's a calling on all of our lives that we must be faithful to.

If you're the one coordinating events at your church or are a part of planning student ministry services, how are you sharing the gospel when you have students gathered together? If students are in your home for Bible study, are you sharing the gospel? We often miss opportunities because "it won't look good if not many people respond" or "we think everyone here knows Jesus." Last time I checked, you and I aren't the Holy Spirit. If He's prompting you to share, do not miss the opportunity. The Holy Spirit does the work—we just have to be willing to tell the story. I love this definition of salvation: "Salvation involves the redemption of the whole man, and is offered freely to all who accept Jesus Christ as Lord and Savior, who by His own blood obtained eternal redemption for the believer. In its broadest sense salvation includes regeneration, justification, sanctification, and glorification. There is no salvation apart from personal faith in Jesus Christ as Lord."[1]

SALVATION

I grew up in church and Christian school, I come from a great family, and it would be easy to say that I've known Jesus my whole life, but that's not true. I made a profession of faith in Jesus Christ when I was seven years old. I remember talking to my parents about my decision and making it public in my church on a Sunday morning. My mom would want me to insert here that when I was in early elementary school, I told her all the time that I loved Jesus and wanted to walk down front at church and tell everyone. My dad was a pastor at our church, and I loved the idea of all eyes being on me, and the church knowing that I loved Jesus as I walked down front during the invitation on Sunday morning. She practically had to stand in front of me to keep me in our pew on Sundays. Good grief! I'm so thankful my parents made sure I understood the decision I was making, and what it all meant.

My mom also said, "You wanted Jesus in your life because our pastor made it sound so good. You wanted whatever someone said would be good." I think this is where a lot of girls are. They want something that sounds good and offers security, so they go for it. I'm not saying you need to question anyone's salvation, but there are ways to help girls understand the gravity and enormity of a relationship with Christ. My parents helped me navigate these waters and said they knew it would be real when I realized I couldn't live without Him. I was a really headstrong little girl who didn't realize she needed Jesus. If you remember the story I told at the beginning of the book of myself as a little girl, that's how I approached life as a kid. I knew best, and I didn't need anyone's help. I had no desire to surrender anything until God captured my heart and began to make me new.

Sanctification is a lifelong process for all Christians, and mine felt like a really slow boil through middle and high school. I remember days when I would have normally been headstrong and defiant, and the Holy Spirit would convict me, and as a result, my behavior would change. I knew salvation was a big deal, and I was sure of my salvation, but it was a series of eye-opening experiences throughout my teen years that God used to show me not just what He saved me FROM, but what He saved me FOR. I began to see there was purpose in all of this, and that God wanted to use me. I began to see things more as not just what

Jesus did for me, but what I can do for Him and His glory. You've heard me share a lot of stories of the women who have discipled me over the years, and they were so critical at these junctures where I needed guidance and help to see and feel the weight of my sinfulness when it was next to the righteousness of Christ, so I could make changes that are still a part of me today.

It really came into play my senior year when I was feeling frustrated and somewhat defiant, and I didn't want to be a part of anything in the student ministry. My parents gave me a long rope that year, so I could learn to make some decisions for myself. They said I didn't have to be a part of my Sunday school class anymore, and through time away, I realized how much I loved and needed my church body. I'm thankful I had the opportunity to figure this out for myself before I left for college. I desperately needed to want church for myself, and not because anyone said I should go.

Through all of these experiences growing up, I came to recognize the enormity of what Christ had done for me, and what surrender to Him looked like. I fell so in love with Jesus in college that I wanted to shout it from the rooftops, because for the first time, I realized the gravity and weight of my sin, and I wanted everyone to know. It was beyond the innocent understandings of a child and teen, and I'm continuing to grow now as an adult.

BAPTISM

Once students begin a relationship with Jesus, baptism is a clear next step of obedience. While it's not a requirement for salvation, baptism is a key step of obedience for anyone who proclaims Jesus as Lord and Savior. We see Jesus commanding this of believers in Matthew 28:19-20, and baptism is also a key part of the story of Philip and the Ethiopian eunuch (Acts 8:36-38). Here's a clear way to put it:

> "Christian baptism is the immersion of a believer in water in the name of the Father, the Son, and the Holy Spirit. It is an act of obedience symbolizing the believer's faith in a crucified, buried, and risen Saviour, the believer's death to sin, the burial of the old life, and the resurrection to walk in newness of life in Christ Jesus. It is a testimony to his faith in the final resurrection of the dead."[2]

You're going to walk with some girls whose lives you will actually see and witness change. There's nothing more beautiful than seeing a life change right in front of your eyes. For other girls (even some who have been in church their whole lives), it's a slower process. You may have a girl say something like this, "I don't want to get baptized—my hair doesn't look good when it's wet!" That's a great opportunity for a follow-up conversation with her to see if she understands what she's learning. If you're terrified of talking about things like the ones we're covering in this chapter, it's okay! Connect with someone on your church staff and have them help you walk through these conversations until you're more comfortable. Let the girls see that you don't always have all the answers.

MAKE DISCIPLES

Discipleship is the next step in the faith walk of every believer. This is why evangelism and discipleship go hand in hand in such a powerful way. Each of these drives the other. When we disciple more believers, they will share their faith with more lost people, who may then become Christians and are in turn discipled. I love it. This is us walking out our faith, and it's the calling placed on the life of every believer.

When we lose sight of the bigger perspective, we often start turning inward and forget our mandate to make disciples.

> Who are some girls in your life who don't have a relationship with Jesus?

> Would you spend a few minutes praying for them by name? And pray God would give you an opportunity to share the gospel with them soon.

> How can you equip the girls in your life to share their faith with their lost friends?

Salvation is about moving from death to life. Darkness to light. It's not something we can skip over or hope someone else talks about so we don't have to. There's a weightiness that comes with these crucial pieces of faith, but there's also an incredible blessing found when girls begin to light up because it's making sense. Encourage the girls you're discipling to share their faith with their friends and family. The more they talk about what God is doing in their lives, the more they'll see all of these pieces coming together. At the end of the day, it's not about checking conversations and things we've done off a list, but letting our lives show the thing we love the most so others can see.

CHAPTER 10

LEAVING A LEGACY

*Show her the way
and embrace the honor
of seeing her show
another the way.*

Let's be real—some of you are just starting out, so maybe you think this chapter doesn't apply to you, but hang in here with me as we wrap this up. One of the most important parts of discipleship is vision for the future.

We may never see the fruit of discipleship this side of heaven. It's often going to be frustrating, sometimes infuriating, and it's always going to cost you something. Discipleship isn't easy. It's an investment. If you're looking for a quick return on your investment, you've missed the point. One of my favorite quotes is by Elton Trueblood, "A man has made at least a start on discovering the meaning of human life when he plants shade trees under which he knows full well he will never sit."[1] Discipleship is like planting a tree. You and I are a part of the process, but we won't always get to sit under that shade tree one day.

One of the most beautiful things to see as a Christian is the legacy of faith from those before us. This is my favorite full-circle story. One year, my cousins Julie and Jody were going with their church to one of the camps my dad helped put together. They had a friend at church named Michael who couldn't afford to go to camp, so my Aunt Jean and Uncle Ronnie paid Michael's camp fees. That summer Michael made a profession of faith and was called to full-time ministry. He was then discipled by our good family friend Wes, who had been an intern under my dad and was serving as the youth pastor at the time. Fast-forward a few years and my brother Rob was in college serving as a leader at a Disciple Now weekend when he heard the speaker was Michael Smith, made the connection back to my dad and Wes, and spoke with Michael. That talk turned into a summer internship for Rob at Michael's church, where he was discipled by Michael.

A couple years later, the church I was serving called a new student pastor who I would serve alongside—it was Michael Smith. While we served together over the next year, he and his wife Kim discipled me. (You read a story from Kim in chapter 7.) So much of what I learned about student ministry I learned from him.

Our obedience matters. The legacy of faith we leave because we are obedient to Christ can and will impact generations. What if my aunt and uncle weren't obedient to help send Michael to camp? What if my brother hadn't taken the initiative to begin a conversation? We aren't responsible for anyone but ourselves, so we have to own our obedience. Nearly ten years ago, Michael unexpectedly passed away because of heart issues, and his funeral was packed. At one point, Wes Searcy asked the crowd, "How many of you were saved as a part of Michael's ministry?" You wouldn't believe how many people stood up. One person made a massive impact, and his legacy lives on in me and so many others.

What will your obedience say about you? It doesn't matter how many lives have been impacted by ours, but that we were obedient with whatever God put before us. I've asked you to answer a lot of questions as you've read this book and given you several challenges to take. My prayer is that God has and will continue to show you what next steps to take. Don't let fear, insecurity, the unknown, or the enemy tell you it doesn't matter and you're not the one. You've been called by a God who will show you the way so you can show her the way.

PRESS ON IN THE JOURNEY

Earlier in the book we talked about Paul and Timothy's journey together, and we looked at several passages from 2 Timothy as Paul was charging Timothy to walk out the calling God had placed on his life. As he wraps up this final letter, he writes:

> *Preach the word; be ready in season and out of season; rebuke, correct, and encourage with great patience and teaching. For the time will come when people will not tolerate sound doctrine, but according to their own desires, will multiply teachers for themselves because they have an itch to hear what they want to hear. They will turn away from hearing the truth and will turn aside to myths. But as for you, exercise self-control in everything, endure hardship, do the work of an evangelist, fulfill your ministry. –2 Timothy 4:2-5*

Now that's a challenge. Here's the deal—you and I have been given the same mission. We know what we're supposed to do, so now we have to take action and put feet to what we know to be true. The more girls establish a relationship with God and know how to love the Lord, the more we are equipping them to be healthy Christ followers for the rest of their lives.

I'll never forget seeing one of my seminary professors (Dr. Allen Jackson) about a year after I graduated. He was in Nashville to film a video and brought along a book he thought I would enjoy. Dr. Jackson was kind enough to write me a note to encourage me in this new season of ministry, and he concluded the note saying, "What you do matters." This short sentence brought tears to my eyes, and it reminded me of the gravity of the work I've been called to. On a regular basis, I pray I feel the weight of the calling God has placed on my life. I don't ever want to forget. I also have passed along that word of encouragement to countless girls ministry leaders and women who are leading teen girls. Let me encourage you with it right now—What you do matters.

LEADING LEADERS

Maybe you're a leader in your church, and you're reading this to try and figure out how to help other leaders catch the vision for discipleship. Can we be best friends? I love that you're trying to help equip others. Discipleship can feel so elusive, and it can be hard to explain. I had a girls ministry brainstorming day with two young ministry leaders, and we spent a couple of hours breaking down discipleship just trying to figure out what the best plan for their leaders and students. It's almost so simple that it's easily overcomplicated. One of the greatest things you can do as a leader is to equip other leaders to come alongside. Multiply your ministry.

When you've got students or leaders who are ready to take the next step, find out what they're looking for. You can make it easy for them by creating some pathways within your ministry that will help point them to the next step. For example, if a student wants to dig deeper into the Bible beyond Sunday mornings, do you have a weekly Bible study group she can plug into? If a student is looking for a mentor, do you have adults who are trained and ready? Maybe the student needs to talk to a counselor—do you have a list in your office or on your phone of local Christian counselors? If she wants to be discipled, ask her what that looks like, so you can point her in the right direction. Because discipleship can happen in a variety of contexts—since it's building relationships and teaching others what you know—be proactive and ready before students start asking.

When you have students gathered together on a Sunday, Wednesday, or whenever your church meets, let them know about other opportunities to connect.

The big question I hear from church leaders is this: Should discipleship be a program, or should it be organic? My answer is yes. You know your church better than anyone else.

What do you think is the best avenue to take?

MULTIPLY

One of the most beautiful parts of discipleship is when we see it multiplied. My friend Anna Townsend is going to share her story of this with you:

ANNA'S STORY

As a freshman in high school, I began a journey that would forever mark and teach me about discipleship. Honestly, when it all began, I didn't realize I was on this journey, but I am grateful for each step along the way.

Alicia was a seventh grade small group leader at my church and served with high school students, too. She spent time getting to know me and my family and would invite me to be a part of special outreach events she did with her seventh graders. One I remember, specifically, was a fall pumpkin carving party she hosted at her house. She invited the girls in her small group and their moms to stop by and enjoy snacks, games, and pumpkin carving art. She asked me to help host the event with her. In the time I'd known her, Alicia observed how I lit up in moments where I got to serve behind the scenes or work with those a little younger than me. I didn't understand then, but she was intentionally creating an opportunity for me to learn what it looked like to serve and get to know others, developing relationships in a fun way.

Then there were DiscipleNow events where Alicia asked me to help collect supplies, pray over the event, or show up early to welcome students. She even asked me to help her develop application activities as we prepared curriculum for the events. There were conversations over a Diet Coke or ice cream, God's Word studied with others, hard talks with sometimes even harder questions to process through. And I know she was praying for me.

In some ways, moments like these taught me what it looked like to model discipleship, to be intentional, to show up in the little and big moments. We are wired for community, to learn and to teach, to give and receive, to point one another to Jesus. Ultimately, God used these moments to draw me to Himself and teach me about the call He placed on my life.

Whether you are called into a discipleship relationship for a season or for a lifetime with someone, know that each moment is significant and matters. Modeling allows her to learn how to pour into someone else. Intentionality establishes trust. Showing up is a physical reminder that we are seen and cared for. All along the way, you are demonstrating that God wired us for relationship. He wired us to invest while being invested in. Show her the way and embrace the honor of seeing her show another the way.

This story is so significant because Anna was still in high school when she learned how to invest in girls younger than her. What girls can you bring alongside of you?

Our call is to multiply. We want to take what we know and add an exponential factor to the process. Once you've led a group, who out of that group is ready to lead and disciple a group of girls? Is there a girl who can lead with you after she's already spent a year with you? How can you multiply your ministry?

Are there other leaders who are asking about what you're doing? Bring them alongside and show them how to disciple! Let your calling and passion for this particular ministry bleed over into every relationship you're a part of. Let other people see the reason you choose to invest your life in others. Discipleship is both caught and taught—we can teach about it all day long, but they have to catch the vision and run with it. Equipping other adults to walk out this step of obedience is critical. It's a calling that is on all of our lives, but some people need to see what it looks like. You be the one who shows them!

Every text you send, phone call you make, passage of Scripture you memorize, or Bible study you lead, all of it builds with each step you take. The Lord uses each piece of investment to build into you and build into those you disciple. One of the greatest blessings of discipleship will be your own personal growth in the Lord. I've learned so much from the girls God has brought into my life over the last decade. They have pushed and challenged me personally, they've asked really hard questions I've had to dig for answers to, and they have encouraged me more than I could ever explain. No one disciples someone else for what they will gain, but the other side is filled with things of which all we can say is, "Only Jesus." He is the One who calls and qualifies us to do what He has called us to do, and He alone gets the glory. We just get to see Him at work and learn as we go. We'll never have full visibility of how God uses what we give back to Him, but we have to trust that He will be faithful with whatever we surrender to Him. Paul reminds us in 1 Thessalonians 5:24, "He who calls you is faithful; he will do it."

Discipleship truly has been one of the greatest joys of my life, both as a discipler and one being discipled. My prayer for you is that you will finish well. That you will give all you have for the name and sake of Jesus because He is worth it. There is nothing glamorous about discipleship. It often uncovers a lot of ugly things, but it's only through Christ that we have a better understanding of how He uses those things for His glory. We all have something to offer if we're willing to open our hands and allow God to use us.

At the end of the day, we have to recognize that Jesus is the way. He is the only way. As we show girls the way, be faithful to show them Jesus.

He is the remedy.

He is the answer.

He is the Way.

John 14:6 says "I am the way, the truth, and the life. No one comes to the Father except through me." We can provide accountability and support, teach and lead girls, but if we weren't in the picture anymore, they need to know it's all about Jesus. Scripture isn't calling you to be an expert, but it's commanding you to show her the Way.

MARY MARGARET RECOMMENDS

. . . .

GIRLS RESOURCES
- *Gen Z: The Culture, Beliefs and Motivations Shaping the Next Generation* - Barna Group
- *Meet Generation Z: Understanding and Reaching the New Post-Christian World* - James Emery White
- *Generation iY* - Dr. Tim Elmore
- *Within Reach*- Ben Trueblood

DEVOTIONALS AND BIBLE READING PLANS
- *All in All Journaling Devotional* - Sophie Hudson
- *Salvaging My Identity* - Rachel Lovingood & Jennifer Mills
- *Foundations: Teen Devotional* - Robby & Kandi Gallaty
- *100 Days* - Angela Sanders
- *Seven Arrows* - Matt & Sarah Rogers

CULTURAL ISSUES:
- *Lies Young Women Believe* - Nancy DeMoss Wolgemuth and Dannah Gresh
- *5 Conversations You Must Have With Your Daughter* - Vicki Courtney
- *A Different College Experience* - Brian Mills & Ben Trueblood

BIBLE STUDIES FOR TEEN GIRLS
- *Seamless* - Angie Smith*
- *The Armor of God* - Priscilla Shirer*
- *The Quest* - Beth Moore*
- *Rachel & Leah* - Nicki Koziarz*
- *Authentic Love* - Amy-Jo Girardier
- *City of Lions* - Amy Byrd

* Studies with asterisks indicate there is also a women's Bible study available

ONLINE HELPS
- lifeway.com/girls

SOURCES

CHAPTER 1

1. Merriam-Webster, "disciple," accessed December 10, 2018, https://www.merriam-webster.com /dictionary/disciple.

2. "Lexicon: Strong's G3101 - mathētēs," Blue Letter Bible, accessed December 10, 2018, https://www.blueletterbible.org/lang/lexicon/lexicon.cfm?Strongs=G3101&t=CSB.

3. Oswald Chambers, "The Service of Passionate Devotion," *My Utmost for His Highest*, accessed December 10, 2018, https://utmost.org/the-service-of-passionate-devotion.

4. N.T. Wright, Paul for Everyone (1 Corinthians) – N.T. Wright – in WordSearch (https://app. wordsearchbible.com), accessed December 10, 2018.

CHAPTER 2

1. Paul David Tripp, *New Morning Mercies: A Daily Gospel Devotional* (Wheaton, IL: Crossway, 2014), 12.

CHAPTER 3

1. Eric Geiger and Jeff Borton, *Simple Student Ministry: A Clear Process for Strategic Youth Discipeship* (Nashville, TN: B&H Publishing, 2009), 12.

2. John Paul Basham, *Be A Man* (Nashville, TN: LifeWay Press, 2015), 9.

3. Ibid, 11.

CHAPTER 5

1. Allen Jackson, *TEACH - The Ordinary Person's Guide to Teaching Students the Bible* (Life Bible Study, 2009), 25.

CHAPTER 8

1. R.C. Sproul, *Essential Truths of the Christian Faith* (Carol Stream, IL: Tyndale House, 2011), 25.

2. Donald Whitney, *Spiritual Disciplines for the Christian Life* (Carol Stream, IL: Tyndale House, 2014), 39-40.

3. "Lexicon: Strong's G3522 - nēsteuō," Blue Letter Bible, accessed December 10, 2018, https://www.blueletterbible.org/lang/lexicon/lexicon.cfm?Strongs=G3522&t=CSB.

CHAPTER 9

1. The 2000 Baptist Faith and Message, "Salvation," accessed December 13, 2018, http://www.sbc.net/bfm2000/bfm2000.asp.

2. The 2000 Baptist Faith and Message, "Baptism," accessed December 13, 2018, http://www.sbc.net/bfm2000/bfm2000.asp.

CHAPTER 10

1. "D. Elton Trueblood Quotes," BrainyQuote, accessed December 10,2018, https://www.brainyquote.com/quotes/d_elton_trueblood_163395.